# Career Coaching Xs and Os

## How to Master the Game of Career Development

mark anthony peterson

© **Copyright 2024 - All rights reserved.**

The content contained within this book may not be reproduced, duplicated or transmitted without direct written permission from the author or the publisher.

Under no circumstances will any blame or legal responsibility be held against the publisher, or author, for any damages, reparation, or monetary loss due to the information contained within this book, either directly or indirectly.

Legal Notice:

This book is copyright protected. It is only for personal use. You cannot amend, distribute, sell, use, quote or paraphrase any part, or the content within this book, without the consent of the author or publisher.

Disclaimer Notice:

Please note the information contained within this document is for educational and entertainment purposes only. All effort has been executed to present accurate, up to date, reliable, complete information. No warranties of any kind are declared or implied. Readers acknowledge that the author is not engaged in the rendering of legal, financial, medical or professional advice. The content within this book has been derived from various sources. Please consult a licensed professional before attempting any techniques outlined in this book.

By reading this document, the reader agrees that under no circumstances is the author responsible for any losses, direct or indirect, that are incurred as a result of the use of the information contained within this document, including, but not limited to, errors, omissions, or inaccuracies.

# Table of Contents

**INTRODUCTION** .................................................................................................. 1
    ABOUT ME .................................................................................................... 1
    A UNIQUE APPROACH ..................................................................................... 2
    WHO WILL BENEFIT ........................................................................................ 2

**CHAPTER 1: HOW TO LAUNCH YOUR CAREER** ................................................. 5
    THE JOB INTERVIEW ........................................................................................ 5
    TIPS TO ACE YOUR INTERVIEWS ...................................................................... 6
        *Informal Interviews* ................................................................................. 6
        *Behavioral Interviews* ............................................................................. 6
        *Case Interviews* ...................................................................................... 7
        *On-the-Spot Interviews* .......................................................................... 8
        *Fit Interviews (Group Interviews)* .......................................................... 8
        *Interview Etiquette* ................................................................................ 8
    THE SIX-MONTH PROBATION PERIOD ............................................................... 9
    TIPS FOR NAVIGATING YOUR PROBATION PERIOD SUCCESSFULLY ................... 10
    FIRST MAJOR COMPETENCY PROJECT ........................................................... 11
    TIPS FOR COMPLETING YOUR FIRST MAJOR COMPETENCY PROJECT SUCCESSFULLY ............. 12
    FIRST MENTOR ............................................................................................. 13
    HOW TO PICK THE RIGHT MENTOR ............................................................... 14
    CHAPTER SUMMARY .................................................................................... 15

**CHAPTER 2: HOW TO BECOME THE MOST PRODUCTIVE MEMBER OF YOUR COMPANY** ...................................................................................................... 17
    HOW YOUR LEADERS NAVIGATE THE SHIP ..................................................... 17
    HOW TO MAKE YOUR WORK COUNT: THE TASK PRIORITIZATION FRAMEWORK ............. 18
    HOW TO LINK YOUR TOP TASKS TO THE COMPANY'S NORTH STAR ................ 19
    HOW TO USE YOUR TOP-PRIORITY TASK METRICS TO CREATE A BALANCE SCORECARD ("BSC") ............. 20
    BUILDING PERSONAL BALANCED SCORECARDS .............................................. 20
    HOW TO ADD LEADING AND LAGGING METRICS TO YOUR BSC ...................... 22
    CHAPTER SUMMARY .................................................................................... 22

**CHAPTER 3: HOW TO MANAGE YOUR MANAGERS** ........................................ 25
    BEING VISIBLE WITHOUT BEING OBNOXIOUS ................................................ 25
    MANAGE YOUR MANAGER .......................................................................... 27
    SKILLS NEEDED TO MANAGE THE MANAGER .................................................. 28

- Building Trust and Communication ............................................. 28
- Developing Influence and Persuasion Skills ................................ 28
- Developing Emotional Intelligence .............................................. 28
- WHAT IF YOU WORK IN A MATRIX ORGANIZATION? ................................. 29
- WHAT IF YOUR BOSS IS YOUNGER THAN YOU? ........................................ 30
- CHAPTER SUMMARY .................................................................................. 31

## CHAPTER 4: HOW TO BUILD AND PROMOTE YOUR BRAND ............ 33

- WHAT IS YOUR CURRENT BRAND AND HOW DO YOU UPGRADE IT FOR SUCCESS? ....... 33
- FINDING A WINNING BRAND ....................................................................... 34
  - Technical Skills ..................................................................................... 34
  - Social Skills ........................................................................................... 35
  - Designing a Roadmap ........................................................................ 35
- FIND A WORK WINGMAN .......................................................................... 36
- PROMOTING YOUR BRAND TO DECISION-MAKERS ...................................... 37
- BE SUPER HUMAN, BUT ALSO BE MORE RELATABLE .................................... 39

## CHAPTER 5: HOW TO GET A RAISE AND BE PROMOTED ................. 43

- ASSESSING YOUR VALUE AND PERFORMANCE ............................................. 44
- PREPARING FOR YOUR PROMOTION ........................................................... 44
  - How to Know if You Are Valued at Work ......................................... 44
  - How to Elevate Your Brand for Promotion ...................................... 45
  - Take on High-Profile Projects ............................................................ 46
  - When to Ask for a Raise/Promotion ................................................. 46
  - How to Negotiate a Raise/Promotion .............................................. 47

## CHAPTER 6: HOW TO BUILD AND MANAGE SUCCESSFUL TEAMS ..... 49

- THE RIGHT PERSON FOR THE RIGHT JOB ..................................................... 49
  - Understanding Employees' Skills ...................................................... 50
  - Understanding What Gives Your Employees Energy ...................... 50
  - Understanding What Diverse Employees Face at Work ................. 51
- BUILDING ACCOUNTABILITY ....................................................................... 51
  - Lead With Transparency .................................................................... 52
  - Report Clear Success Metrics ............................................................. 52
  - Assign Meaningful Success Metrics to Each Team Member .......... 52
  - Celebrate Success ................................................................................ 52
  - Transitioning Unsuccessful Employees in a Respectful Manner .... 53

## CHAPTER 7: HOW TO NETWORK AND SUPERCHARGE YOUR MENTOR RELATIONSHIPS ............................................................. 55

- THE 3 PS OF NETWORKING ........................................................................ 55
  - People .................................................................................................. 56
  - Purpose ................................................................................................ 56
  - Pathways ............................................................................................. 57

SKILLS/CHARACTERISTICS REQUIRED FOR SUCCESSFUL NETWORKING ............................ 58
    *Active Listening* ............................................................................................ 58
    *Positive Attitude* .......................................................................................... 58
    *Empathy* ...................................................................................................... 59
    *Approachable* .............................................................................................. 59
    *Giving* .......................................................................................................... 59
BUILDING YOUR COUNCIL OF MENTORS ................................................................ 60
NURTURE YOUR NETWORK ................................................................................... 61
    *Regular Communication* ............................................................................. 62
    *Personalized Interactions* ........................................................................... 62
    *Celebrate Milestones and Achievements* .................................................... 62
    *Engage in Mutual Support* .......................................................................... 62
    *Preserve Memories and Maintain Connections* ......................................... 63
    *Utilize Technology and Social Media* .......................................................... 63

**CHAPTER 8: HOW TO NAVIGATE CORPORATE SOCIAL GATHERINGS .............. 65**

DRAWBACKS TO NOT ATTENDING CORPORATE EVENTS ........................................ 65
    *Negative Brand Impressions* ....................................................................... 66
    *Limited Knowledge and Skills Development* .............................................. 66
    *Limited Exposure and Visibility* ................................................................... 66
    *Missed Personal Connections* ..................................................................... 66
    *Limited Access to Mentorship* .................................................................... 67
    *Missed Business Opportunities* ................................................................... 67
GETTING NOTICED AT CORPORATE EVENTS *WITHOUT* BEING THE LIFE OF THE PARTY ......... 67
    *Prepare and Set Goals* ................................................................................ 67
    *Dress and Present Professionally* ................................................................ 68
    *Engage in Meaningful Conversations* ......................................................... 68
    *Demonstrate Expertise* ............................................................................... 68
    *Actively Participate in Sessions* ................................................................... 68
    *Utilize Social Media* .................................................................................... 68
    *Volunteer or Offer Assistance* ..................................................................... 69
    *Follow Up After the Event* .......................................................................... 69

**CHAPTER 9: HOW TO MANAGE A PERSONAL CRISIS WITHOUT DERAILING YOUR CORPORATE CAREER .................................................................................... 71**

STAYING PRODUCTIVE WHEN YOU HAVE A PERSONAL CRISIS ............................... 72
HOW TO TELL YOUR MANAGER YOU ARE DEALING WITH A PERSONAL CRISIS ............. 74

**CHAPTER 10: WALK A MILE IN SOMEONE'S SHOES—HOW TO LEAD DIVERSE TEAMS ........................................................................................................... 77**

DIVERSITY VS. DIFFERENCE VS. WOKE .................................................................... 77
    *Diversity* ...................................................................................................... 78
    *Difference* ................................................................................................... 78
    *Woke* .......................................................................................................... 78

- Why Diversity Is Essential in Corporate America .................................................. 79
  - *Increased Innovation and Creativity.............................................................79*
  - *Broader Market Reach ...............................................................................80*
  - *Enhanced Decision-Making and Problem-Solving ........................................80*
  - *Increased Employee Engagement and Retention........................................80*
- Seeing Through Different Eyes.................................................................. 80
- How to Lead a Diverse Team—Manager Self-Assessment ...................... 82

## CHAPTER 11: HOW TO BREAKUP WITH YOUR EMPLOYER AND REMAIN FRIENDS ............................................................................................................85

- How to Know When It Is Time to Leave Your Company .......................... 86
- How to Notify Your Manager When You Are Ready to Quit................... 88
- How to Thank Your Company Mentors Before You Leave...................... 89

## CHAPTER 12: YOU ARE READY TO LEAVE CORPORATE AMERICA TO BECOME AN ENTREPRENEUR—WHAT'S YOUR NEXT MOVE? ......................................................91

- Corporate Perks: Join Every Corporate Rewards Program *Before* You Quit Your Job ................................................................................................................ 92
- Soft Launch Your Startup While Maintaining Corporate Job............................ 93
- Startup Checklist .............................................................................................. 95

## CONCLUSION .................................................................................................99

- Resources for New Corporate Employees ......................................................... 99
- Mental Health Resources ................................................................................. 99
- Career and Leadership Book Recommendations............................................. 100
- Startup Resources ........................................................................................... 102

## GLOSSARY....................................................................................................105

## REFERENCES................................................................................................109

# Introduction

In the fast-paced and competitive world of corporate America, young employees face numerous obstacles and challenges that threaten to hinder their progress. Navigating these barriers effectively requires the knowledge and skills akin to mastering a complex game where the rules are often unwritten, the strategies elusive, and the outcomes significantly impact one's professional trajectory. This playbook and tactical guide are meticulously crafted to equip aspiring professionals with the tools they need to prevail in the face of adversity and achieve remarkable success.

## About Me

Allow me to introduce myself. My name is Mark A. Peterson, and I am honored to be your guide on this fascinating journey. As the founder and CEO of the Techstars and Google-backed startup Ziscuit, Inc., I have witnessed firsthand the real-life challenges that young employees confront daily. Ziscuit strives to eliminate food insecurity and food deserts through innovative grocery retail solutions, providing me valuable experience tackling corporate hurdles head-on.

With more than two decades of senior executive experience spanning various industries—food, consulting, data, and biometrics—I have encountered the trials and tribulations of climbing the corporate ladder. However, my passion for entrepreneurship has always burned bright, leading me to embark on several ventures since my high school and college days. My previous book, *Guerrillapreneur: Small Business Strategy for Davids Wanting to Defeat Goliath*s, shared my insights and tips on succeeding against corporate giants.

As an extension of my commitment to empowering individuals on their professional journeys, I also host the highly acclaimed podcast

*Career Coaching Xs and Os.* Through the podcast, I have had the privilege of connecting with countless driven individuals seeking enlightenment and guidance on the path to career mastery. Now, with the culmination of my experiences, successes, and failures, I proudly present this comprehensive guide to career development—an invaluable resource for anyone aspiring to rise above the obstacles and reach their full potential.

## A Unique Approach

At this point, you may wonder what sets this book apart from the countless others in the career development genre. This guide stands out amidst the noise as a definitive playbook—unearthing the secrets, tactics, and strategies necessary to thrive within the modern corporate landscape.

Drawing from my extensive background in diverse industries, I have distilled decades of acquired knowledge into an actionable framework that delivers actual results. This book is not a mere collection of theoretical concepts; it is a practical guide providing you with precisely what you need to know to overcome the most daunting challenges in your pursuit of professional growth. Consider it your secret weapon—a playbook that demystifies the inner workings of corporations, unveiling the hidden game that transpires behind the metaphorical curtain of the Wizard of Oz. Armed with this knowledge, you will possess a distinct advantage, enabling you to outmaneuver your competitors and leap ahead in your career trajectory.

## Who Will Benefit

This book primarily aims to empower and enlighten college and graduate-school students eager to dive headfirst into the corporate world. These ambitious individuals seek to embark on their careers with confidence and accelerate their progression by acquiring the insider knowledge that eludes so many. They yearn for the secrets that lie beneath the surface—secrets that can give them the crucial edge needed to surmount the obstacles ahead.

Whether you are an ambitious student about to embark on your first professional endeavor or a seasoned professional seeking to reclaim control over your career trajectory, this book will serve as a compass to navigate the treacherous waters of corporate America. By guiding you through each stage of the game, from understanding the rules to strategically maneuvering through setbacks, *Career Coaching Xs and Os* will empower you to unlock your full potential and master the game of career development. You will also learn how to make an impression at your workplace. If you want a preview, here's a [podcast](#) that's just right for you.

Let's explore the intricate strategies and tactics that will reshape your understanding of career development and usher you toward unparalleled success. The journey awaits, and the Xs and Os are ready to be mastered. Let's step onto the field together and rewrite the rules of the game.

# Chapter 1:
# How to Launch Your Career

*We cannot solve our problems with the same thinking we used when we created them.*
–Albert Einstein

Starting your career can be overwhelming. The decisions you make, the people you meet, and the experiences you gain in the early stages of your professional life can profoundly impact your future. It's important to understand that launching your career is like launching a startup. You only have so much runway, and if you don't use your resources correctly, you'll run out of time and opportunities.

In this chapter, we'll focus on the steps you need to take to successfully launch your career, including (1) acing the job interview, (2) navigating the six-month probation period, (3) completing the first major competency project, and (4) finding your first mentor. By the end of this chapter, you'll learn how to navigate these gates and set yourself apart from other candidates and employees.

## The Job Interview

The job interview gate is the first step in launching your career. Companies use different types of interviews based on the industry and department you wish to join. One of the most common types of interviews is the informal, or get-to-know-you, interview. This interview is designed to assess your personality, work experience, and interests. Behavioral interviews focus on your past experiences to determine how you would handle specific scenarios. Case interviews test problem-solving skills by presenting you with a real-life business problem. Competency interviews test your skills related to the job requirements. On-the-spot interviews occur when you have not scheduled an interview but happen to meet an interviewer. Finally, fit interviews (group interviews) allow for several candidates to be screened at once in a group setting. In my podcast, *Career Coaching Xs and Os*, I discuss five things you shouldn't do during an interview.

## Tips to Ace Your Interviews

### *Informal Interviews*

*Interview goal: To test your genuine interest in the company and to assess your job qualifications*

- Read the Annual Report or 10K to learn about the company.

- Boil your résumé down to a 60-second elevator speech. Focus on relevant skills and job positions.

- Confirm company dress code and match the interviewer's energy.

## Behavioral Interviews

*Interview goal: To confirm your participation in the experiences and achievements listed on your résumé*

- Use the STAR method (Situation, Task, Action, Result) to structure your responses (Massachusetts Institute of Technology, 2022).

- Focus on showcasing your skills and abilities through real-life examples.

- Highlight your problem-solving, teamwork, and communication skills.

## Case Interviews

*Interview goal: To assess your analytical and reasoning skills and in a realistic business setting (Consulting, 2023)*

- Interviewers care more about how structured your thinking is than the right answer.

- Interviewers also want to know if you know where to find the data needed to answer the question.

- Ask clarifying questions and seek additional information, if needed.

## Competency Interviews

*Interview goal: A competency-based interview assesses a candidate's strengths and weaknesses in the key competencies required by the role*

- Prepare examples of situations in which you demonstrated these competencies.

- Explain your thought process and how you arrived at certain decisions or outcomes.

- Show enthusiasm and motivation aligned with the job requirements.

## On-the-Spot Interviews

*Interview goal: To give the employer a better sense of the candidate's true character and capabilities without giving the candidate time to prepare or rehearse their answers (Lewis, 2023)*

- Prepare for questions with constraints or that probe your weaknesses, such as describing yourself in one word or stating how many times you have failed.

- Focus on maintaining a positive attitude and showcasing your adaptable nature.

- Don't be afraid to ask for clarification if you need more time to answer a question.

## Fit Interviews (Group Interviews)

*Interview goal: To assess whether your qualities are compatible with the company's culture*

- Show collaborative and team-oriented behavior during group exercises.

- Actively listen to and engage with other candidates during group discussions.

- Highlight your ability to work well in a team and contribute to a positive work environment.

## Interview Etiquette

Displaying the right Interview etiquette can separate you from other candidates and help you secure the job, especially if the hiring manager is "old-school." Here are some essential tips you should consider:

- Wear a suit to the interview. No one ever lost a job for being overdressed. It shows you are serious about the job.

- When entering the manager's office, *never* sit before the manager and let them sit first. I always ask if I can be seated. It shows that you have respect and understand the office hierarchy.

- Always bring a portfolio to take handwritten notes. Sure, you can use your phone to take notes, but again, for old-school hiring managers, the old ways are the best ways.

- Bring enough paper copies of your résumé for people interviewing you.

- Never call anyone by their first name until given permission to do so.

- Always send a follow-up "Thank You" email to everyone who participated in your interviews. Old ways die hard, and many of the decision-makers in major corporations still believe that the little things matter.

## The Six-Month Probation Period

The second gate is the six-month probation period. During this period, you are expected to prove your worth to the company. Unfortunately, many new hires make mistakes that can harm their career prospects. Some common mistakes include taking a vacation, being late for work or leaving early, asking for personal time off, missing team and corporate events, and missing deadlines. To avoid these mistakes, you need to prioritize your work, understand company culture, and communicate effectively with your manager and team.

# Tips for Navigating Your Probation Period Successfully

- **Understand expectations.** Make sure you clearly understand the company's expectations and the job responsibilities during this period. Before starting the task, seek clarification from your manager and ask for advice from your team's top performer. If I played backup quarterback for the Patriots in the early 2000s, I would have picked Tom Brady's brain before I did anything on the field.

- **Build strong relationships.** Make an effort to build positive relationships with your colleagues, supervisors, and other key stakeholders by offering to assist them with their projects. Collaboration and teamwork can help you navigate the probation period successfully.

- **Communication is key.** Keep open lines of communication with your supervisor. Seek feedback regularly to understand how you are performing and if there are any areas for improvement. If your supervisor has the capacity, ask for a bi-weekly 30-minute mentoring meeting. Make sure you have an agenda for each meeting.

- **Set clear goals.** Discuss and set clear goals with your supervisor at the beginning of the probation period. This will help you stay focused and track your progress throughout the period.

- **Demonstrate commitment.** Show dedication, enthusiasm, and a willingness to learn. Be proactive in seeking out opportunities to grow and develop in your role.

- **Seek training and support.** Take advantage of any training programs or resources available. This shows your commitment to learning and improving in your role.

- **Adapt to company culture.** Understand and adapt to the company culture and values. This means that you should not use phrases like "At my last company" or "My last boss didn't do it that way." Allow yourself to learn how things are done at this company *before* you start offering advice.

- **Take initiative.** Find ways to contribute beyond your immediate responsibilities—e.g., offer to help with the company's charitable events. Show initiative and take on new projects or responsibilities when possible.

- **Seek feedback and reflect.** Regularly reflect on your performance and seek feedback from your supervisor and peers. Use this feedback to make improvements and address any areas of concern.

- **Stay positive and don't give up.** The probation period can be challenging, but stay positive and persistent. Complainers are the first people fired in tough times. Use any setbacks as an opportunity for growth and learning. It is critical that you avoid all the potholes in corporate America. Take the time to listen to the Top Five Mistakes New Employees Make in Corporate America on my podcast.

# First Major Competency Project

The third gate is the first major individual and team competency project. Completing this project can be daunting, but it's also an opportunity to showcase your skills and that you work well within a team. We'll take an in-depth look at the steps you can take to ensure you deliver an exceptional project. These steps include understanding the project details and scope, prioritizing tasks, delegating effectively, communicating frequently and clearly with your team, and confidently presenting your final product.

# Tips for Completing Your First Major Competency Project Successfully

- **Understand the project requirements.** Begin by thoroughly understanding the project requirements, including the goals, deliverables, and timeline. Ask any clarifying questions to ensure you have a clear understanding.

- **Break down the project.** Break the project into smaller tasks and create a detailed project plan or timeline. This will help you stay organized and track your progress throughout the project.

- **Research and gather information.** Conduct thorough research related to the project to gather the necessary information. Use reliable sources and ensure that you have a comprehensive understanding of the topic.

- **Seek guidance and support.** If you have any questions or uncertainties during the project, seek guidance from your supervisor or mentor. They can provide valuable insights and help you navigate any challenges.

- **Develop a strategy.** Create a strategy or framework for approaching the project. Determine the steps you will take and the methodologies you will use to complete each aspect successfully.

- **Use your skills and knowledge.** Apply your skills, knowledge, and expertise to the project. This is an opportunity to showcase your abilities and demonstrate your competency.

- **Collaborate with others.** If the project requires collaboration, actively engage with team members and stakeholders. Foster positive relationships and effectively communicate to ensure smooth coordination and successful outcomes.

- **Manage your time effectively.** Set specific deadlines for each task and manage your time efficiently. Prioritize your work and create a work schedule that allows you to meet the project requirements.

- **Regularly review and reflect.** Continuously review your progress and reflect on your work. Assess whether you are on track and if any adjustments or improvements need to be made.

- **Seek feedback and iterate.** Throughout the project, seek feedback from your supervisor or mentor. Use this feedback to make necessary adjustments and iterations to enhance the quality of your work.

- **Quality assurance.** Prioritize quality and attention to detail in your deliverables. Review your work for errors or areas for improvement. Ensure that your final project meets the desired standards.

- **Learn from the experience.** Once the project is complete, reflect on the experience and identify lessons learned. Consider how you can apply these insights to future projects and enhance your competency even further. Now that you have completed your first project, listen to my podcast episode on how to become Indispensable at work.

# First Mentor

Finally, securing your first mentor can be a game-changer when launching your career. A mentor can offer advice, support, and guidance as you navigate the early stages of your professional life. However, finding the right mentor can be challenging. We'll discuss how to seek out senior members of your team and tenured employees with your job title in another group.

# How to Pick the Right Mentor

- **Identify your goals.** Clarify your career goals and the specific areas where you would like guidance and support. Having clear objectives will help you find a mentor who aligns with your needs.

- **Research potential mentors.** Look for individuals within your organization with the knowledge, experience, and skills you want to develop. Consider their expertise, track record, and compatibility with your values and working style.

- **Seek compatibility.** A successful mentorship relies on a good personal and professional fit. Look for someone with whom you have chemistry and whose personality and communication style resonate with you.

- **Network and build relationships.** Engage in networking opportunities and build relationships with potential mentors. Attend industry events, join professional associations, and participate in networking groups to increase your chances of connecting with suitable mentors.

- **Approach mentors thoughtfully.** Once you have identified potential mentors, approach them respectfully and explain why you believe they would be a valuable mentor to you. Express your admiration for their work and share your specific goals and aspirations.

- **Establish mutual benefits.** Recognize that mentorship should be mutually beneficial. Show how your mentorship can provide value to the potential mentor, such as gaining insights into generational perspectives or learning from your unique skill set.

- **Be proactive and show initiative.** Take the initiative to schedule meetings or interactions with your mentor and come prepared with specific questions or topics for discussion. Show that you are committed and eager to learn.

- **Be open and receptive.** Be open to feedback, constructive criticism, and new perspectives that your mentor offers. Demonstrate a willingness to learn from their experiences and implement their guidance.

- **Maintain regular communication.** Regularly update your mentor on your progress and seek their advice on your challenges or decisions. Schedule regular check-ins or meetings to maintain a consistent and fruitful relationship.

- **Show appreciation.** Recognize and express appreciation for the time, effort, and guidance your mentor provides. Show gratitude through small gestures, such as a thank you note or a token of appreciation.

## Chapter Summary

As I conclude this chapter, it is important to remember that starting out may feel daunting, but with the right mindset, skills, and determination, you can pave a successful path for yourself. Embrace the challenges, seize opportunities, and always continue to learn and grow. Now, let's turn our attention to the next chapter, where we will explore how to become the most productive member of your company.

In the next chapter, we will delve into the strategies and practices that will empower you to become the most productive member of your company. From mastering time-management techniques to honing your communication skills, we will explore the key factors contributing to workplace efficiency and effectiveness. Get ready to unlock your full potential and stand out as a valuable asset to your organization. Before you move ahead, don't forget to check out my podcast on <u>things you should avoid</u>.

## Chapter 2:
# How to Become the Most Productive Member of Your Company

*The least productive people are usually the ones who are most in favor of holding meetings.*
—Thomas Sowell

In today's fast-paced business world, productivity is the name of the game. Companies are constantly searching for ways to improve efficiency. To put yourself on the fast track to the top, you need to make sure that the majority of the work you do is connected to what makes the company succeed. But how can you achieve this? In this chapter, we will discuss how to eliminate non-value-adding tasks and how to align your work with your company's success metrics.

# How Your Leaders Navigate the Ship

Successful athletes follow metric-driven training routines to improve their performance. You need to use the same approach to become a high-performance employee. Runners track their miles, and baseball players track their batting averages. What should you track? The first step you should take in determining which metrics you should track is to find out what your company's "North Star" Performance Indicator ("North Star") is. The North Star is the metric leadership used to determine whether the company is succeeding year-over-year. For instance, Facebook's North Star includes Reach, Impressions, Likes, and Comments, whereas Coca-Cola's North Star includes Revenue and Economic Value-Added (EVA). When you have a clear understanding of the company's North Star, you can prioritize your work tasks into four buckets: (1) "Top-Priority tasks," (2) "Stretch-Goal tasks," (3) "Tasks to Automate," and (4) "Tasks to Outsource."

# How to Make Your Work Count: The Task Prioritization Framework

The Task Prioritization 2X2 framework is designed to help you prioritize your tasks into one of the four buckets listed above. The y-axis (top-to-bottom) measures how much the tasks differentiate your company. The x-axis (right-to-left) measures how much the tasks improve your company's North Star performance.

# TASK PRIORIZATION FRAMEWORK

|  | Tasks To Automate | Top Priority Tasks |
|---|---|---|
| **Differentiates Company from Competitors** (− to +) | Tasks To Outsource | Stretch Goal Tasks |

**Improves North Star Performance** (− to +)

Map your current job tasks using the Task Prioritization framework by asking two questions: "Does this task help differentiate my company from our competitors?" and "Does this task improve my company's operating performance?" Tasks that differentiate and improve North Star's performance are your top-priority tasks. Tasks that *do not* differentiate but *do* improve North Star's performance are your stretch-goal tasks. Tasks that *do not* differentiate and *do not* improve North Star's performance are tasks that *must* be outsourced or eliminated. (Note: You will get big brownie points from your boss if you produce cost savings by eliminating needless tasks.) Tasks that *do not* improve North Star's performance but differentiate the company should be automated so that they require as little of your time as possible. When you finish mapping your tasks using this framework, you will be one step closer to becoming the Usain Bolt of your office.

# How to Link Your Top Tasks to the Company's North Star

Now that you have defined your top-priority tasks, you need to align those tasks with three to five metrics that measure your weekly performance. Remember, top long-distance runners measure the number of miles run and the speed per mile. How should you measure your Top Priority task productivity? Review <u>this article on work metrics</u> and use it as a starting point for creating a list of metrics to measure your work. Our ultimate goal is to build a balanced scorecard that will be your weekly playbook.

Note: When you become a manager, you will use these same frameworks to manage your team.

# How to Use Your Top-Priority Task Metrics to Create a Balance Scorecard ("BSC")

What is a balanced scorecard ("BSC")? It is a tool created by professors Robert S. Kaplan and David Norton in their famous article in the *Harvard Business Review* in 1992 titled "The Balanced Scorecard: Measures that drive performance" (Johnson et al., n.d.). A BSC measures past performance data and provides feedback on making better decisions in the future. A traditional BSC includes metrics from four areas: financial, customer, operations, and employee learning and growth.

To create your BSC, you should start by cataloging all the metrics related to your top-priority tasks and separating them into one of the four areas. Click this link if you need to see an example of the type of metrics used by high-performance employees.

## Building Personal Balanced Scorecards

The personal balanced scorecard, inspired by the business management tool, allows individuals to assess their lives, set priorities, and set goals for the future. The scorecard consists of four verticals: financial health, physical health, professional achievement, and personal relationships. These categories represent key areas of life that contribute to overall well-being and success.

One of the unique aspects of the personal balanced scorecard is its semi-annual approach. By reviewing progress at regular intervals, individuals can make necessary adjustments and course corrections throughout the year. This approach ensures that there is enough time to make changes and align actions with desired outcomes.

It's important to note that while the personal balanced scorecard provides a structured framework for evaluation, it is not a one-size-fits-all solution. Goals and metrics may vary depending on individual circumstances and priorities. The scorecard should be customized to reflect personal values; aspirations; and specific, measurable, and meaningful targets.

The process of building a personal balanced scorecard helps individuals clarify their priorities and gain a deeper understanding of what truly matters to them. It encourages individuals to set specific goals that can be measured while also acknowledging that not everything of value can be easily quantified.

It's worth mentioning that there may be differing opinions on the use of such scorecards in personal life. Some argue that focusing on time management and goal orientation could detract from the enjoyment of living in the present moment. However, many find value in the process of setting priorities, tracking progress, and aligning actions with their vision for a fulfilling and balanced life.

| Balanced Scorecard Project<br>Measurement Lag / Lead Comparison | | | |
|---|---|---|---|
| | Strategic Objective | Lag / Outcome Measure | Lead / Driver Measure |
| Financial | | *Most of your financial measures are outcomes* | |
| Customer | | *Most of your customer measures are outcomes* | |
| Processes | | *Mix of outcomes* | *and drivers* |
| L & G | | | *Most of your Learning and Growth measures will be drivers* |

Comments:
A good balanced scorecard should consist of both outcome and driver type measurements. The two upper perspectives (Financial and Customer) will have mostly outcome type measurements. The lower two perspectives (Internal Processes and Learning & Growth) will include some driver type measurements. The Learning & Growth perspective may include several driver type measurements. This worksheet categorizes your measurements and compares the two types of measurements

# How to Add Leading and Lagging Metrics to Your BSC

A distinction exists between leading and lagging indicators in assessing performance. While leading indicators look forward to predicting future outcomes and trends, lagging indicators look back to determine achieved outcomes. The difference between the indicators is akin to driving a car—leading indicators are like looking through the windshield at the road ahead, while the lagging indicators are similar to looking through the rear window at the road you've already traveled.

Business has several examples of leading indicators useful for predicting future outcomes. These include new product pipeline, brand recognition, growth in new markets or sales channels, and customer or employee satisfaction. Your role is to assist leaders in predicting likely future outcomes for the business. This will help ensure the company stays ahead of the pack and is well-prepared for the future. Additionally, you can use lagging indicators to understand past performance, identify areas of improvement, and benchmark the organization against industry standards. Examples of these indicators include revenue, profit, and revenue growth.

## Chapter Summary

By implementing the strategies and techniques discussed in this chapter, you can position yourself as a highly productive member of your company. Remember, productivity is not just about working harder but also about working smarter and focusing on the most important tasks. By continuously improving your skills, managing your time effectively, and adopting a proactive mindset, you can significantly impact your performance and contribute to the success of your organization.

In the next chapter, we will shift our focus from being a productive employee to effectively managing your managers. Developing strong relationships with your superiors becomes crucial as you progress in your career. We will explore strategies for effective communication, building trust, setting expectations, and navigating power dynamics. Learn how to manage and create a productive working relationship with your managers to enhance your career trajectory and achieve your professional goals. Stay tuned for valuable insights and practical tips in the next chapter.

# Chapter 3:
# How to Manage Your Managers

*Employees who were never competent are promoted to management to limit the damage they can do.*
–Dilbert

In today's corporate landscape, organizations are complex entities comprised of various tribes vying for resources and leadership positions. Among these tribes, one relationship stands out as crucially important—that between an employee and their manager. Managers play a pivotal role in guiding and influencing the success of their team members, while employees, on the other hand, have the power to shape and manage their managers. This delicate balance of power and influence is the essence of managing managers effectively.

Managing one's manager may seem counterintuitive to traditional hierarchical structures within organizations. However, with the increasing emphasis on collaboration, empowerment, and personal growth, it has become imperative for employees to take an active role in shaping their working relationships. This chapter aims to explore the strategies, principles, and skills required to manage managers successfully.

## Being Visible Without Being Obnoxious

Before you can manage your manager, you have to make yourself visible, i.e., showcase your talents. Being visible in the workplace is important for career advancement and recognition. However, it is equally important to strike a balance and avoid appearing obnoxious or attention-seeking. Here are some strategies to be visible without being obnoxious:

- **Focus on delivering quality work.** The foundation of being noticed for your work is consistently producing high-quality results. Instead of seeking attention directly, put your energy into ensuring that your job stands out for its excellence. This will naturally draw attention and make your contributions more noticeable.

- **Communicate your achievements.** While it's important to avoid bragging, it's equally important to let others know about your accomplishments. Find appropriate opportunities to communicate your achievements to your boss and colleagues. When discussing your successes, frame them in a way that highlights their impact on the team or organization as a whole rather than solely focusing on yourself.

- **Participate in team activities and initiatives.** Actively participate in team meetings, projects, and initiatives. Contribute your insights, ideas, and expertise in a collaborative manner.

- **Volunteer for additional responsibilities.** Look for opportunities to take on additional responsibilities that align with your skills and interests. This demonstrates your willingness to go above and beyond and allows you to showcase your capabilities to a wider audience. However, make sure to balance the workload and not take on too much, as it may negatively impact the quality of your work.

- **Build positive relationships.** Developing strong relationships with your boss and colleagues is essential for getting noticed. Be respectful, supportive, and collaborative with your coworkers. Offer help, share your knowledge, and contribute to a positive work environment. Building relationships based on trust and respect can lead to more visibility and opportunities for advancement. If you need additional help getting noticed by your boss, check out Episode 1 of my podcast, "Five Ways To Get Noticed By Your Boss."

- **Seek feedback and guidance.** Continuous improvement is important for professional growth. Seek constructive feedback from your boss and colleagues to understand areas where you can enhance your skills and performance. This not only helps you improve but also demonstrates your commitment to personal development, which can gain recognition.

- **Utilize appropriate communication channels.** Be mindful of how you communicate your achievements. Utilize appropriate communication channels, such as team meetings, status reports, or performance reviews, to share your accomplishments. This ensures that you are being visible in a professional and respectful way.

# Manage Your Manager

Acknowledging the complexities within the manager-employee relationship is vital to fully comprehend the dynamics behind managing managers. While managers are positioned as leaders within the organizational hierarchy, they also rely on their subordinates for success. Employees possess valuable knowledge, insights, and perspectives that can be harnessed to enhance individual and team performance. The ability to manage one's manager requires an understanding of this symbiotic relationship and the recognition that employees can contribute significantly to their manager's effectiveness.

Managing upwards is a key aspect of managing managers effectively. This involves proactively anticipating the needs and preferences of their manager, aligning their work to support their manager's goals, and providing timely updates and information to keep them informed.

# Skills Needed to Manage the Manager

## Building Trust and Communication

Trust and effective communication form the bedrock of any successful relationship, including that between employees and their managers. To manage their managers effectively, employees must establish trust through transparency, reliability, and integrity. Building trust requires open and honest communication, active listening, and transparency in sharing concerns, ideas, and feedback.

## Developing Influence and Persuasion Skills

Being able to influence and persuade one's manager is a critical skill for managing managers. Employees need to possess the ability to articulate their ideas, present logical arguments, and navigate through differing viewpoints to gain support for their initiatives. Developing these skills involves understanding the motivations and interests of their manager, tailoring messages to resonate with their preferences, and building coalitions to garner support for their proposals.

## Developing Emotional Intelligence

Emotional intelligence is a critical skill for managing managers (Out, 2023). This entails the ability to understand, manage, and regulate one's emotions while effectively interpreting and responding to the emotions of others. By developing emotional intelligence, employees can navigate their managers' various personalities and leadership styles, adapting their approach to ensure effective communication and collaboration. Emotional intelligence also allows employees to handle conflicts and disagreements constructively and respectfully, ultimately enhancing the overall relationship.

# What if You Work in a Matrix Organization?

Escaping the matrix or navigating a matrix management structure in a corporate environment is essential for career growth and advancement. In a matrix organization, employees often report to multiple bosses across different teams or departments, making it crucial to manage expectations and build positive relationships with each of them. Here are some strategies to consider:

- **Clarify roles and responsibilities.** Understand the specific expectations and responsibilities associated with each of your bosses. Request meetings or discussions to discuss your roles in each team and seek clarity on their priorities.

- **Communicate openly and proactively.** Regular and effective communication is key when working in a matrix management structure. Keep your bosses informed about your progress, challenges, and achievements. Be proactive in sharing updates and seek their guidance and feedback.

- **Adapt to different management styles.** Different bosses may have distinct management styles and preferences. Take the time to understand these differences and adjust your approach accordingly. Pay attention to how each boss likes to receive information, their preferred communication channels, and their priorities.

- **Establish clear objectives and deliverables.** Work with each boss to establish clear goals, objectives, and deliverables. This will provide a framework for success and allow you to manage expectations on both sides. Regularly review progress towards these objectives and communicate any potential delays or challenges promptly.

- **Build relationships and seek feedback.** Take the initiative to build positive relationships with each of your bosses. Schedule one-on-one meetings to discuss your goals, performance, and any areas where you can improve. Seek their feedback and guidance on how to excel in your role.

- **Develop your networking skills.** In a matrix management structure, networking is crucial to your success. Take the opportunity to connect with colleagues across teams and departments.

# What if Your Boss Is Younger Than You?

Dealing with a generational gap between you and your boss can present unique challenges in the workplace. However, with the right approach, you can manage the age difference and make a <u>positive impression on your younger supervisor</u>. Here are some strategies to consider:

- **Seek common ground.** While there may be differences in age and generational experiences, there are often shared interests and values that can form the basis of a connection. Look for common ground, such as shared hobbies, industry trends, or work-related goals.

- **Be open to new perspectives.** Recognize that your younger boss may have different experiences and ideas. Be open-minded and willing to learn from their insights.

- **Embrace technology and digital skills.** Younger generations often have a strong grasp of technology and digital tools. Take the initiative to improve your digital literacy skills and be open to adopting new technologies in your work.

- **Show your experience and expertise.** While your boss might be younger, you likely have accumulated a wealth of experience and expertise in your field. Look for opportunities to showcase your knowledge and contribute to the success of projects or initiatives.

- **Foster open and respectful communication.** Effective communication is crucial in any workplace relationship, regardless of the generational gap. Be intentional about establishing open lines of communication with your boss, seeking their input, and providing constructive feedback when needed.

- **Embrace continuous learning and growth.** Commit to ongoing learning and professional development. Stay current with industry trends, attend relevant workshops or conferences, and seek opportunities for growth within your organization. By continuously investing in your development, you demonstrate your commitment to self-improvement, which can be <u>noticed and appreciated</u> by your younger boss.

- **Be supportive and collaborative.** Offer your support and mentorship to your younger boss when appropriate. Share your experiences, insights, and lessons learned. By being a supportive and collaborative team member, you can build a positive relationship that transcends any generational gap.

# Chapter Summary

As we conclude this chapter, it's clear that effective leadership is an essential skill for any professional. By understanding the dynamics of your organization, establishing open communication channels, and providing guidance and support, you can empower your managers to thrive and drive success. But management is just the beginning of building a lasting and influential career.

The upcoming chapter will explore the fascinating world of brand building and promotion. Your brand is your unique identity in the professional landscape, and it has the power to differentiate you from the competition. We will uncover powerful techniques to craft and communicate your brand story effectively, showcase your strengths, and create a lasting impression with key stakeholders. Join us as we unravel the secrets to building a strong personal brand and leveraging it to advance your career. Get ready to unlock your full potential and leave a lasting impact.

# Chapter 4:
# How to Build and Promote Your Brand

*Too many people overvalue what they are not and undervalue what they are.*
–Malcolm Forbes

Establishing a strong and recognizable personal brand is crucial for professional success and advancement in today's social media–driven business world. Your brand is not just a logo or a tagline; it embodies who you are, what you stand for, and how you differentiate yourself from others in your field. Building and promoting your brand effectively can open up numerous opportunities, enhance your credibility, and help you stand out in a crowded marketplace.

This chapter aims to provide you with practical strategies, tips, and insights on how to build a strong personal brand from the ground up and promote it effectively across various platforms. From defining your brand identity to crafting a compelling narrative; from leveraging digital channels to networking strategically, this chapter will equip you with the knowledge and tools you need to create a lasting impression and leave a mark in your industry.

## What Is Your Current Brand and How Do You Upgrade It for Success?

One valuable approach to effectively assessing and improving your current brand is to utilize 360-degree feedback. This feedback mechanism involves gathering input from various sources—such as supervisors, colleagues, direct reports, and even clients—to comprehensively understand how you are perceived in the professional environment.

Receiving feedback from multiple perspectives can give you a well-rounded view of your strengths, areas for improvement, and how others perceive your brand. This feedback can shed light on aspects of your brand that you may not have been aware of or highlight blind spots that could be hindering your professional growth. You can use several tools to get feedback. First, you can send a simple email soliciting feedback. Second, build a Google Table. This tool can help you tabulate and analyze the data. Finally, you can pay for 360-degree feedback tools.

The next step in upgrading your brand for success in conducting a brand gap analysis. This process involves benchmarking your brand against successful employees within your organization or industry. By comparing your brand attributes, behaviors, and achievements with those of top performers, you can identify gaps and opportunities for enhancement.

To conduct a brand gap analysis, define the key success factors or competencies valued in your field. Make sure the factors you select are measurable and easily tracked. These may include metrics that define an individual's brand. For example, if you are building your brand around software development, you may want to measure your "code stability" relative to the top performers in your department. Next, gather data on how you currently stack up against these success factors through self-assessment and feedback from others.

# Finding a Winning Brand

## *Technical Skills*

Technical skills are specific abilities and knowledge related to a particular job or industry. These skills are typically measurable and can be acquired through education, training, or experience. To identify the technical skills most valued at your company, you will want to consult job descriptions, speak with colleagues, or conduct research on industry trends.

For example, in a technology company, technical skills such as programming languages, data analysis, cloud computing, or cybersecurity may be highly valued. In a marketing firm, skills such as digital marketing, SEO optimization, analytics, or graphic design may be sought after. Assess the technical skills that are highly valued in your company and evaluate your current proficiency in those areas.

## *Social Skills*

In addition to technical skills, social skills, also known as soft skills or people skills, play a crucial role in building a winning brand. These skills encompass aspects such as communication, teamwork, leadership, adaptability, emotional intelligence, and problem-solving abilities. They are more difficult to quantify but are highly valued by employers, as they contribute to a positive work environment and effective collaboration.

To identify the social skills most valued at your company, observe the behaviors and traits exhibited by respected and successful colleagues. Notice the qualities that are praised or recognized in the workplace, such as effective communication, active listening, empathy, or the ability to build and maintain relationships.

## *Designing a Roadmap*

Once you have identified the technical and social skills most valued at your company, you need to create a roadmap for obtaining these skills and integrate them into your brand.

Start by conducting a self-assessment to evaluate your current proficiency in the identified skills. Identify areas where you excel and areas where improvement is needed. Determine which skills are most critical for your desired career path and set specific goals for acquiring or enhancing them.

Consider various learning opportunities to develop these skills, such as attending workshops, enrolling in courses or certifications, seeking out mentors or coaches, or taking on challenging projects that allow you to practice and refine the identified skills.

## Find a Work Wingman

A work wingman supports and advocates for your professional growth and success in the workplace. They can be a colleague, mentor, or even a friend who understands your goals and is willing to help you achieve them. A work wingman can be incredibly valuable in advancing your career and opening new opportunities.

To find a work wingman, start by identifying individuals in your workplace who have similar career goals or are in positions you aspire to. Look for someone successful, well-connected, and respected within the organization. Building a strong professional relationship with this person will be the foundation for a successful work-wingman partnership.

Next, approach the potential work wingman, express your admiration for their achievements, and ask if they would be willing to mentor or guide you in your career. Be genuine and explain why you believe they would be a valuable ally. You need to establish trust and mutual respect from the beginning.

Your work wingman can play a vital role in promoting your career by:

- **Providing guidance and advice:** Your work wingman can offer valuable insights and suggestions on navigating the professional landscape. They can share their experiences, offer feedback on your performance, and help you set realistic goals.

- **Introducing you to influential people:** Having a well-connected work wingman can open doors to new opportunities. They can introduce you to key individuals within your organization, industry, or professional network who can help you advance your career.

- **Recommending you for projects or promotions:** Your work wingman can advocate for you when seeking new projects, promotions, or career development opportunities. They can vouch for your skills, experience, and potential, increasing your visibility and chances of success.

- **Acting as a sounding board:** Your work wingman can provide valuable insight and perspective on important decisions or challenges you may face. They can help you weigh the pros and cons, identify potential risks, and provide support when making difficult choices.

- **Boosting your confidence and morale:** Having a work wingman who believes in your abilities can be incredibly motivating. They can provide encouragement, celebrate your achievements, and offer support during setbacks or challenging times.

## Promoting Your Brand to Decision-Makers

Promoting your brand to decision-makers is crucial for the success of your business. Decision-makers are the key individuals or groups responsible for making important choices related to investments, partnerships, and purchases. These individuals include executives, managers, board members, or purchasing agents. Effectively promoting your brand to decision-makers requires a delicate balance between showcasing your strengths and unique value proposition without coming across as bragging. Here are some strategies to promote your brand without appearing boastful:

- **Understand your target audience.** Before promoting your brand, you should thoroughly understand your target audience, including decision-makers. Research their backgrounds, interests, challenges, and goals. This will help you tailor your messages and choose the most appropriate platforms for promotion.

- **Focus on providing value.** Instead of boasting about your brand, concentrate on the value and benefits you and your brand provide to decision-makers. Understand their pain points and highlight how your brand can effectively solve their problems and meet their needs.

- **Utilize case studies and testimonials.** Decision-makers are often more influenced by evidence and real-life success stories than direct claims. Using case studies and testimonials from satisfied customers can help demonstrate the value of your brand without bragging. Highlight how your brand has positively impacted the businesses or organizations of others.

- **Establish thought leadership.** Becoming a thought leader in your industry can significantly enhance your brand's credibility without resorting to bragging. Share your expertise through creating valuable content, such as blog posts, articles, or white papers, that address relevant industry challenges.

- **Network strategically.** Attend industry conferences, seminars, or networking events where decision-makers are likely to be present. Engage in conversations without pushing your brand aggressively. Instead, focus on building meaningful connections, listening to their challenges, and offering valuable insights.

- **Leverage social media.** Social media platforms provide an effective and cost-efficient way to reach decision-makers. Share engaging and informative content that highlights your brand's expertise and solutions. Engage with decision-makers by commenting on their posts, sharing content, and participating in relevant industry discussions.

- **Participate in industry events.** Speaking at industry conferences or hosting webinars positions your brand as an expert. Rather than focusing solely on self-promotion, provide valuable insights and practical solutions to common industry challenges. Decision-makers will be more receptive to your brand if they view you as a knowledgeable resource, not just someone promoting themselves.

- **Collaborate with influencers or industry experts.** Partnering with influencers or respected industry experts can help amplify your brand's reach and credibility. When influential individuals endorse your brand or collaborate with you on content, decision-makers are more likely to pay attention.

## Be Super Human, But Also Be More Relatable

Being superhuman and relatable at the same time can be a powerful combination, when it comes to making friends and influencing executives. One effective way to achieve this balance is by using self-deprecating humor. Self-deprecating humor involves making lighthearted jokes or comments about oneself in a way that brings laughter and builds connections with others. Here's how you can use self-deprecating humor to make friends and influence executives:

- **Show humility.** Executives and influential individuals are often accustomed to dealing with people who put them on a pedestal. By using self-deprecating humor, you can break down that barrier and show you're humble and down-to-earth.

- **Find common ground.** Self-deprecating humor allows you to connect with others by highlighting shared experiences or struggles. By making jokes about your mistakes or shortcomings, you create an opening for others to relate and share their stories.

- **Lighten the mood.** Executives and decision-makers are often under significant pressure, so being able to inject some humor into a conversation can help alleviate tension and create a more relaxed atmosphere. Self-deprecating humor can be a powerful tool to break the ice, make people feel at ease, and create a more receptive environment for your influence.

- **Avoid arrogance.** Arrogance and self-promotion can be off-putting, especially to executives who are used to being approached by individuals seeking to impress them or gain their favor. By using self-deprecating humor, you demonstrate that you don't take yourself too seriously and are willing to laugh at your imperfections.

- **Share relatable stories.** Use self-deprecating humor to accompany stories or anecdotes that are relatable to the executives you're trying to influence. When you can make light of your mistakes or foibles while highlighting a valuable lesson learned, it creates a memorable and relatable experience for your audience.

- **Use in moderation.** While self-deprecating humor can be a powerful tool, use it in moderation and gauge the appropriateness of the situation. Overusing self-deprecating humor can give the impression that you lack confidence or undermine your abilities. It's important to strike a balance between humor and being taken seriously, especially when dealing with high-level executives.

- **Read the room.** Pay attention to the reactions and cues from executives and adjust your approach accordingly. Not everyone may appreciate or respond well to self-deprecating humor, so it's important to be sensitive to the context and the individuals involved. If you sense that your humor is not being well received, it's best to steer the conversation toward a different approach.

Building and promoting your brand is a multifaceted process that requires careful planning, consistent effort, and practical strategies. You can establish a strong and compelling brand presence by understanding your target audience, showcasing your unique value proposition, and leveraging various promotional channels.

Now that you have successfully built and promoted your brand, it's time to focus on your professional growth and advancement. The next chapter will explore proven strategies and techniques to help you navigate the corporate landscape and position yourself for a raise and a promotion. From showcasing your accomplishments to developing strong relationships within your organization, get ready to unlock the secrets to climbing the corporate ladder and achieving your career goals.

# Chapter 5:
# How to Get a Raise and Be Promoted

*"You don't get paid for the hour. You get paid for the value you bring to the hour."*
–Jim Rohn

In today's competitive professional landscape, individuals aspire to grow in their careers and improve their financial prospects. When it comes to career advancement, one of the most sought-after goals is getting a raise or a promotion. While the thought of securing a higher salary or a more prestigious position may be enticing, achieving these milestones requires effort, strategy, and the ability to effectively negotiate your worth. In this chapter, we will explore the principles and techniques that can help you <u>navigate the path to securing a raise and promotion</u>.

Before we delve into the strategies, it is crucial to address a fundamental principle put forth by author Chester Karras: "In business as in life, you don't get what you deserve. You get what you negotiate. Simply desiring a raise or a promotion will not guarantee success. To increase your chances, you must focus on generating more value than you are currently being compensated for" (Karrass, 1996). This key takeaway sets the tone for this chapter; it is not merely about asking for more money or a better title but about demonstrating your ability to contribute to the organization in a way that justifies the investment.

# Assessing Your Value and Performance

To successfully position yourself for a raise or a promotion, an essential first step is objectively evaluating your value and performance. This involves assessing your skills, expertise, accomplishments, and contributions to the organization. Consider the impact you have made, both quantitatively and qualitatively, on projects, team performance, and overall organizational goals. Understanding your value will provide you with the confidence needed for negotiations and enable you to clearly articulate your accomplishments to your superiors. You may remember the balanced scorecard from Chapter 2. It will help assess your performance and overall value.

Note: This simple question can help determine whether you are building a value-driven career: "Can my team/department survive a month without my contributions?" If the answer is yes, you have not made yourself indispensable.

# Preparing for Your Promotion

## *How to Know if You Are Valued at Work*

- **Recognition and feedback:** If your superiors regularly acknowledge and appreciate your work, provide constructive feedback, and seek your input, it is a clear sign that you are valued.

- **Responsibilities and assignments:** Being entrusted with challenging tasks and important projects implies that your capabilities and contributions are respected.

- **Inclusion and involvement:** Being invited to crucial meetings, decision-making processes, or strategic discussions indicates that your opinions and expertise are highly regarded.

- **Development opportunities:** If your organization invests in your professional growth through training, mentorship, or additional responsibilities, it demonstrates that they value your potential.

- **Collaboration and teamwork:** Your colleagues and supervisors seeking your collaboration and valuing your input during team projects or problem-solving activities indicate that your contributions are esteemed.

## How to Elevate Your Brand for Promotion

- **Define your unique value proposition.** Identify your strengths, skills, and expertise that set you apart. Articulate them clearly to emphasize your exceptional value.

- **Showcase your achievements.** Publicize your accomplishments by documenting them in a portfolio, sharing success stories with colleagues, or presenting them during team meetings.

- **Enhance your skills.** Constantly upgrade and develop new skills that align with your job role or industry trends. Continuous learning displays your commitment to growth and adds value to your brand.

- **Build a strong professional network.** Connect with industry professionals, attend conferences/seminars, and actively participate in relevant communities. A robust network enhances your visibility and credibility.

- **Create an online presence.** Use platforms like LinkedIn or personal websites to display your expertise, share insights, and establish yourself as a thought leader.

- **Seek endorsements and recommendations.** Request testimonials or endorsements from colleagues, clients, or industry experts who can vouch for your skills and expertise.

## *Take on High-Profile Projects*

- **Express interest and willingness.** Speak to your supervisor to highlight your interest in working on high-profile projects and how they align with your career goals and professional growth.

- **Showcase relevant skills and experience.** Demonstrate that you possess the necessary skills and knowledge to handle the project successfully. Highlight past experiences that apply to the project's requirements.

- **Build credibility and trust.** Consistently deliver high-quality work on your existing assignments. This builds trust among your superiors and increases the chances of being considered for high-profile projects.

- **Seek mentorship.** Approach a senior colleague or someone experienced in the field who can guide you and vouch for your capabilities. Their support can significantly increase your chances of being selected for such projects.

## *When to Ask for a Raise/Promotion*

- **Achieving significant milestones:** If you have accomplished outstanding results, attained challenging targets, or successfully completed high-impact projects, it may be an appropriate time to ask for a raise or a promotion.

- **Positive performance reviews:** If you consistently receive positive feedback, exceptional performance ratings, or are recognized for your achievements, it indicates that you are ready for advancement.

- **Increased responsibilities:** When you have taken on additional responsibilities or have shown exceptional growth in your role, you are ready for a higher position and compensation.

- **Market research:** Stay updated with industry standards and salaries for similar positions. If you find that you are being underpaid compared to the market, it could be a valid reason to discuss a raise.

- **Time frame:** Evaluate whether you have been in your current role for a reasonable time to justify considering a raise or a promotion. It typically varies by industry, but around 1–2 years is a common timeframe.

## How to Negotiate a Raise/Promotion

- **Prepare and research.** Gather information about industry standards, salary ranges, and the value you bring to the organization. Have a clear understanding of your goals and ideal outcomes before entering negotiations.

- **Highlight accomplishments.** Present a comprehensive list of your achievements, contributions, and impact on the organization. Emphasize how these justify a raise or a promotion.

- **Present a business case.** Articulate how your skills, experience, and expertise add value to the organization and align with its goals. Show how a raise or a promotion would benefit both parties.

- **Consider alternative options.** If a raise is not immediately feasible, explore alternative benefits like additional vacation days, flexible working arrangements, professional development opportunities, or performance-based bonuses.

- **Be confident and professional.** Maintain a calm and assertive demeanor throughout the negotiation. Clearly express your expectations and be open to compromise and alternative solutions.

- **Practice active listening.** Understand the employer's perspective and concerns. Engage in a constructive dialogue to find a mutually beneficial solution.

- **Follow up.** After the negotiation, thank the person involved and seek clarity on any next steps or timelines.

Understanding when and how to ask for a raise or a promotion can significantly impact your career growth and financial well-being. By recognizing your value, demonstrating your worth, and negotiating effectively, you can increase your chances of receiving the recognition and advancement you deserve. Now, let's focus on another crucial aspect of professional success: building and managing successful teams.

The next chapter looks at the art of building and managing successful teams. From fostering collaboration and effective communication to leveraging diverse strengths and resolving conflicts, we will explore the key strategies and skills required to create high-performing teams that drive organizational success.

## Chapter 6:
# How to Build and Manage Successful Teams

*Management is about persuading people to do things they do not want to do, while leadership is about inspiring people to do things they never thought they could.*
—Steve Jobs

If you are reading this chapter, you have gotten your promotion and have been assigned a team to lead. Building and managing successful teams are essential for the success of any organization. Teams that work well together can achieve remarkable results, surpassing individual efforts and accomplishments. In today's competitive business environment, companies are increasingly relying on teams to accomplish complex tasks, solve problems, and drive innovation.

The success of a team depends on the clear alignment of goals, strategies, and values among team members, as well as the removal of barriers that hinder collaboration and communication. The goal of this chapter is to provide insights, strategies, and practical tips on how to build and manage successful teams, with an emphasis on creating a winning culture and establishing a clear "line of sight" for team members.

# The Right Person for the Right Job

When it comes to building and managing successful teams, one crucial aspect is ensuring that employees are in the right roles within the organization. Each individual has unique skills, strengths, and personalities that make them better-suited for certain tasks or roles. The concept of "Stop trying to make an apple an orange" emphasizes the importance of recognizing these individual differences and matching employees with the right job roles to maximize their potential and productivity.

## *Understanding Employees' Skills*

To effectively put employees in the right job roles, leaders and managers need to have a deep understanding of each individual's skills, capabilities, and areas of expertise. This involves conducting skill assessments, performance evaluations, and regular feedback sessions to identify strengths and areas for development. By recognizing what each employee excels at and where they may need support, managers can align responsibilities and tasks that play to their strengths, ultimately leading to improved job satisfaction and performance. Top companies like Google use a variety of ways to test employee skill levels, including psychometric tests (measures cognitive ability), cognitive aptitude (measures general intelligence), and situational judgment (problem-solving). You may not have the funds to test team members this extensively, but you certainly want to review past performance before you assign roles on the team.

## Understanding What Gives Your Employees Energy

Another element of assigning employees to appropriate job roles entails comprehending their sources of motivation and energy. The Myers-Briggs Type Indicator (MBTI) is a widely used personality assessment tool that classifies individuals into distinct personality types based on their preferences in four critical domains: Introversion/Extraversion, Sensing/Intuition, Thinking/Feeling, and Judging/Perceiving. By understanding employees' MBTI types, managers can obtain valuable insights into their communication styles, work preferences, decision-making approaches, and sources of motivation.

For example, employees with introverted preferences may prefer to work independently or in smaller groups, while those with extraverted preferences may thrive in collaborative settings. Employees with a preference for thinking may prioritize logical reasoning and objectivity in decision-making, while those with a feeling preference may prioritize empathy and harmony in interpersonal relationships.

## Understanding What Diverse Employees Face at Work

In today's diverse workforce, leaders and managers need to recognize and address the unique challenges and experiences that employees from diverse backgrounds may face in the workplace. Diversity encompasses differences in race, ethnicity, gender, age, sexual orientation, physical abilities, and more. Managers must proactively create an inclusive and supportive environment where all employees feel valued, respected, and empowered to contribute their perspectives and talents.

By understanding the <u>challenges that diverse employees may encounter</u>, such as unconscious bias, microaggressions, or lack of representation, leaders can implement strategies to promote diversity, equity, and inclusion within the team. This may include providing diversity training, mentoring programs, affinity groups, and inclusive policies that celebrate and leverage the strengths of a diverse workforce.

# Building Accountability

Building a culture of accountability within an organization requires a comprehensive approach that includes transparency, clear communication, setting meaningful success metrics, celebrating achievements, and managing underperforming employees respectfully. Here is a detailed overview of each aspect:

## Lead With Transparency

Leading with transparency means creating an environment where information is shared openly and honestly. This helps in building trust among team members and encourages accountability. Leaders should communicate openly about the organization's goals, challenges, and progress. Transparent communication helps employees understand their roles and responsibilities and how their contributions impact the overall success of the organization.

## Report Clear Success Metrics

Defining clear success metrics is crucial for holding individuals and teams accountable. Success metrics should be specific, measurable, achievable, relevant, and time-bound (SMART). By clearly defining key performance indicators (KPIs) and goals, team members have a clear understanding of what is expected from them. Regularly reporting on these metrics helps track progress, identify areas for improvement, and celebrate achievements.

## Assign Meaningful Success Metrics to Each Team Member

Assigning meaningful success metrics to each team member involves aligning individual goals with the broader objectives of the organization. By setting personalized targets and expectations, employees are more likely to take ownership of their work and be accountable for their performance. Team members must be involved in the goal-setting process to ensure that their goals are realistic and motivating and that they contribute to the overall success of the team.

## Celebrate Success

Celebrating success is an essential aspect of fostering a culture of accountability. Recognizing and rewarding achievements, both big and small, motivates employees to maintain high performance levels and reinforces positive behavior. Celebrating success can take various forms, such as public recognition, rewards, team activities, or performance bonuses.

## *Transitioning Unsuccessful Employees in a Respectful Manner*

Despite efforts to build a culture of accountability, there could be instances where employees are unable to meet expectations or perform at the required level. In such cases, you need to address performance issues promptly and respectfully. Leaders should have <u>open and honest conversations with underperforming employees</u> to identify underlying causes and provide support or additional resources, if needed. If performance does not improve, transitioning employees out of the organization should be done with empathy and professionalism, ensuring that the process is fair, transparent, and respectful.

Building and managing successful teams is a complex, yet rewarding, process that requires a combination of effective leadership, clear communication, and fostering a culture of accountability. By implementing the strategies discussed in this chapter, organizations can create high-performing teams that drive growth and achieve outstanding results.

In the next chapter, we will look at the power of networking and mentor relationships. Discover how to leverage your professional connections, build a strong network, and maximize the benefits of mentorship to accelerate your career growth and unlock new opportunities. Get ready to take your professional relationships to the next level!

# Chapter 7:
# How to Network and Supercharge Your Mentor Relationships

*"You can have everything in life you want if you will just help enough other people get what they want"*
–Zig Ziglar

Networking is an essential skill that can enable people to succeed in their careers and lives. This skill involves forming meaningful relationships with others, leading to mutual benefits that can contribute to personal and professional growth. The above quote embodies this principle, emphasizing the importance of helping others before helping oneself.

The primary goal of this chapter is to help individuals understand the importance of networking and mentorship and how it can lead to personal and professional success. A key takeaway from this chapter is that networking is not about selfishly pursuing personal gain but, instead, about helping others first.

# The 3 Ps of Networking

Learning to network effectively is critical to building valuable professional relationships that can open doors to new opportunities and support personal and career growth. The 3 Ps of networking—people, purpose, and pathways—provide a comprehensive framework for understanding and maximizing the benefits of networking.

## *People*

The first P of networking emphasizes the importance of connecting with the right *people*. It involves identifying individuals who can provide value, guidance, and support based on their expertise, experience, or industry connections. Building a strong network starts with being intentional about the relationships you want to form.

When considering the "people" aspect of networking, casting a broad net beyond your immediate circle is essential. Aim to diversify your network to access a variety of resources, knowledge, and opportunities. Remember the adage that "If you are the smartest person in the room, find a different room with smarter people." The first thing 19-year-old LeBron James did after joining the NBA was to meet with Warren Buffett, the smartest investor and one of the richest men in the world. Thirty years later, LeBron James is a billionaire.

Building genuine relationships is crucial. Approach networking as you would approach a first date. Make sure you do your research on the individual before you meet. Write down 3–5 ways you can advance their career. These notes will help you ensure that your initial interactions are successful.

Note: The best networkers consistently capture notes about the people they meet. I capture my notes in Excel and update them each time I learn new information about one of my connections.

## *Purpose*

The second P in networking is having a *purpose* that serves as a strategic guide for your networking activities. It helps you define the types of people you need to connect with and the resources or opportunities you should seek. For example, if you want to transition into a new industry, networking with professionals already established in that field can provide valuable insights and potential job leads.

Your purpose may evolve as your career or personal goals change. Regularly assess your objectives and adjust your networking approach accordingly. By aligning your purpose with your networking efforts, you can make meaningful connections and increase the likelihood of achieving your desired outcomes.

Note: Some individuals create a vision board to express their purpose. Here is a link to an underline article about vision boards.

## *Pathways*

The third P of networking, *pathways*, refers to the various channels and approaches you can use to connect with the right people and achieve your networking goals.

Pathways for networking can be both traditional and digital. Traditional pathways include attending industry conferences, seminars, or local professional events. These physical gatherings provide face-to-face opportunities to build personal connections. Keep an updated wish list of conferences you want to attend each year. Submit your list to your boss and see if your company has the training dollars to send you. Proactive employees get funded first.

In the digital age, online networking platforms have become increasingly influential. The number of companies reviewing your social media accounts before extending an offer is increasing. Social media platforms like LinkedIn offer a vast network of professionals you can connect with, but more and more companies are leveraging platforms like Facebook, YouTube, Reddit, X, and TikTok to connect with potential hires, vendors, and customers. Your first action as a corporate employee is to audit all your social media accounts. Eliminate *everything* that contradicts the personal brand you are building.

# Skills/Characteristics Required for Successful Networking

Successful networking requires a combination of skills and characteristics that can help individuals build meaningful connections and foster mutually beneficial relationships. Here are some essential skills and characteristics for successful networking:

## *Active Listening*

Active listening is a crucial skill for networking. It involves hearing what the other person is saying and paying attention to their body language, tone of voice, and underlying meaning. The Three As of active listening are attentive, awareness, and amiable. Attentive listeners are focused and make mental notes. Aware listeners are cognizant of the context. Imagine listening to Dr. King's "I Have a Dream Speech" without knowing the context of the time. The impact will be lost on you. Amiable listeners maintain a positive attitude even if they disagree with what's being said.

## *Positive Attitude*

Maintaining a positive attitude is vital for successful networking. A positive mindset helps individuals approach networking opportunities with enthusiasm, optimism, and an open mind. It allows individuals to create a positive impression on others and creates a sense of trust and likeability. A positive attitude also enables individuals to handle setbacks, rejection, or challenges in networking with resilience and determination.

## *Empathy*

Empathy is the ability to understand and share the feelings, thoughts, and experiences of others. It is a crucial characteristic for successful networking, as it allows individuals to connect on a deeper level with the people they interact with. In one of his commercials promoting The General Insurance, brand ambassador and 7-foot tall former NBA player Shaquille O'Neal walks in shoes belonging to a female half his height. As O'Neal's feet break through the shoes several sizes too small, he remarks, "It is hard to walk a mile in someone else's shoes." If you are unwilling to walk in someone else's shoes, you are not ready to network.

## *Approachable*

Being approachable is a crucial characteristic for successful networking. It involves creating an inviting and welcoming presence that encourages others to initiate conversations and connections. Approachable individuals are friendly and open and display positive body language, making it easier for others to feel comfortable approaching them. Taylor Swift, arguably one of the most famous people on the planet, was a fixture at Kansas City Chiefs football games during the 2023/24 season. Nearly every post I read about people who met included the word "approachable." I credit this common touch as a reason she is loved globally.

## *Giving*

Networking is not just about taking or self-promotion. Successful networkers have a give-first attitude. Sharing knowledge, offering assistance, and making introductions to others are examples of giving behaviors that strengthen networking relationships. Giving also fosters reciprocity, where others are more willing to support and assist in return.

# Building Your Council of Mentors

Networking to find your council of mentors is a strategic approach to building a supportive and diverse group of mentors who can guide you in various aspects of your personal and professional life. A council of mentors provides you with different perspectives, insights, and expertise, helping you navigate challenges, make informed decisions, and grow as an individual. Here are some steps to consider when networking to find your council of mentors:

- **Identify your needs and goals.** Start by identifying your specific needs and goals. What areas do you seek guidance and support in? This could range from career development, entrepreneurship, personal growth, leadership, or any other relevant aspect. Determining your goals will help clarify the type of mentors you seek and the network you need to build.

- **Leverage existing connections.** Tap into your existing network to find potential mentors. This includes colleagues, supervisors, professors, alumni, community leaders, or people you have met through professional or social activities. Reach out to individuals who have experience or expertise in areas aligned with your needs and goals. Inform them about your desire to develop a council of mentors and inquire if they would be interested in becoming part of it or if they can recommend someone suitable.

- **Attend networking events and conferences.** Participate in industry-specific networking events, conferences, or seminars where you can meet professionals who excel in fields of interest. Engaging with like-minded individuals provides an opportunity to establish connections that could lead to mentorship opportunities. Be proactive in approaching people and expressing your interest in learning from their experiences. Exchange contact information and follow up with personalized messages to maintain the connection.

- **Join professional associations or organizations.** Become a member of professional associations or organizations related to your field. These platforms provide networking opportunities and access to a pool of experienced professionals who can serve as mentors. Attend meetings, workshops, or webinars organized by these associations to engage with potential mentors and build relationships based on shared interests and goals.

- **Seek mentors through mentorship programs.** Many universities, corporations, and nonprofit organizations offer mentorship programs that connect mentees with mentors from various backgrounds. Explore these programs and apply to become a mentee. These structured programs often provide guidance and resources to support mentor-mentee relationships. It's an excellent way to find mentors who can provide specific guidance in your areas of interest.

- **Utilize online platforms.** Online platforms like LinkedIn, industry-specific forums, or mentorship platforms can be powerful tools for finding mentors. Join relevant online communities, participate in discussions, engage with industry leaders, and leverage these platforms to seek mentorship opportunities. Reach out to professionals who inspire you or have the experience you seek, and express your interest in learning from them.

# Nurture Your Network

Nurturing your network is essential in building and maintaining strong relationships. Whether they're personal or professional connections, actively investing in these relationships helps foster trust, support, and future opportunities. Here are some key strategies to consider:

## Regular Communication

Regularly staying in touch with your network is critical to nurturing those relationships. This can be done through various channels, such as phone calls, emails, video chats, or social media platforms. Carve out time to catch up, share updates, and show genuine interest in their lives. Consistency is key to keeping the connection alive and building a sense of mutual support.

## Personalized Interactions

When interacting with your network, make an effort to personalize your conversations. Remember and reference specific details from previous interactions, such as their interests, achievements, or challenges they mentioned. Show that you genuinely care about their well-being and growth. Personalized interactions create a deeper and more meaningful connection, making your network feel valued and appreciated.

## Celebrate Milestones and Achievements

Another way to nurture your network is by celebrating milestones and achievements. Congratulate your network members on their successes, whether it's a promotion, a new job, an award, or a personal accomplishment. Acknowledging their achievements makes them feel good and demonstrates your support and encouragement. This can strengthen the bond and create a positive impression of you as a reliable and supportive contact.

## Engage in Mutual Support

Nurturing your network is a two-way street. Show your willingness to support others by offering assistance, sharing resources, or making introductions when appropriate. Actively listen and provide helpful feedback or advice when needed. By being an active and supportive member of your network, you develop a culture of trust and reciprocity, making it more likely for others to reciprocate the support and nurture the relationship.

## *Preserve Memories and Maintain Connections*

Keeping memories fresh is essential in preserving the shared experiences and moments you've had with your network. Share photos, videos, or articles that remind you of shared experiences. Revisiting those memories can reignite the connection and serve as a basis for future conversations and meetings. Additionally, make an effort to attend events or gatherings where you can physically meet and spend quality time with your network, strengthening the personal bond.

## *Utilize Technology and Social Media*

In this digital era, technology and social media platforms offer excellent tools for nurturing your network. Stay connected through platforms like LinkedIn, which allow you to post updates, engage in discussions, and congratulate others on their achievements. Use tools like calendars and reminders to schedule follow-ups and check-ins. Online networking events and webinars can also provide opportunities to connect with new individuals and expand your network.

The next chapter will focus on navigating corporate social gatherings. From office parties to networking events, corporate social gatherings offer opportunities to build relationships and establish yourself as a valuable team member. We will discuss strategies to navigate and make the most of these events, including tips on networking, building connections, and having a presence that leaves a lasting impression.

# Chapter 8:
# How to Navigate Corporate Social Gatherings

*Here's to fooling your company into thinking that you are mature enough to handle an open bar.*
–Anonymous

Navigating corporate social gatherings can be a delicate balancing act. On the one hand, these events provide valuable networking opportunities, a chance to build relationships with colleagues, and a platform to showcase your professionalism. On the other hand, there's a fine line between making a positive impression and unintentionally crossing boundaries that could tarnish your reputation in the corporate world. Understanding the nuances of corporate social gatherings and mastering the art of navigating them with finesse is crucial for corporate success.

This chapter will equip you with the knowledge and skills needed to navigate corporate social gatherings with confidence, grace, and professionalism. Whether it's an office party, a networking event, or a corporate dinner, mastering the art of navigating these gatherings can set you apart and contribute to your success in the professional world.

## Drawbacks to Not Attending Corporate Events

While there are many benefits to attending corporate events, there are also several drawbacks to not attending them.

### *Negative Brand Impressions*

In Chapter 4, we discussed the importance of building a personal brand. Skipping corporate events is a surefire way to destroy your brand. First, you may be labeled negatively for missing the events. Second, if you are not present at events, who will speak up or defend you should your name get mentioned during conversations? Being invisible is never a good thing in corporate America.

### *Limited Knowledge and Skills Development*

Corporate events often provide valuable learning experiences through workshops, seminars, and panel discussions. Not attending these events means missing out on the opportunity to gain new knowledge, learn about industry trends, and enhance professional skills.

### *Limited Exposure and Visibility*

Corporate events act as a platform for professionals to showcase their expertise, gain exposure, and enhance their professional reputation. By not attending these events, individuals miss the chance to present themselves as thought leaders or subject-matter experts in their field.

## *Missed Personal Connections*

Conversations will inevitably turn to your personal life at corporate events. Your boss may learn that your kids attend the same school or that you grew up in the same town as his grandparents. According to CNBC, "up to 80% of jobs are filled through personal connections" (Lopez, 2023).

## *Limited Access to Mentorship*

Corporate events are a prime opportunity to connect with potential mentors who can provide guidance and support in one's career. By not attending these events, individuals miss out on building strong professional relationships with mentors who can offer valuable advice, share experiences, and help shape their career trajectory.

## *Missed Business Opportunities*

These events are not just about networking; they're also about exploring potential business opportunities and partnerships. By not attending, individuals may miss out on discovering new prospects, forging collaborations, or strengthening existing business relationships, resulting in a loss of potential growth and expansion.

# Getting Noticed at Corporate Events *Without* Being the Life of the Party

Getting noticed at corporate events without being the life of the party is still possible by focusing on a few key strategies. Here are some practical ways to stand out and make a positive impression:

## *Prepare and Set Goals*

Before attending the event, set clear goals for what you want to achieve. This could include connecting with specific individuals, learning about certain topics, or seeking specific opportunities. By coming prepared and focused, you can make intentional interactions to help you stand out.

## Dress and Present Professionally

Your attire and overall presentation can make a significant impact. Dress appropriately for the event, ensuring your clothing is professional, well-fitting, and reflects the nature of the event. Maintaining good posture, eye contact, and a confident demeanor will also help you project a professional image.

## Engage in Meaningful Conversations

Instead of trying to engage in small talk with everyone, focus on having meaningful conversations with a few select individuals. Listen actively, show genuine interest, and ask thoughtful questions. This will demonstrate your engagement and make a lasting impression on those you speak with.

## Demonstrate Expertise

Leverage your knowledge and expertise in conversations whenever possible. Share valuable insights, offer solutions to industry challenges, or discuss recent trends. This will establish you as a knowledgeable professional and position you as a valuable resource.

## Actively Participate in Sessions

During workshops, panels, or Q&A sessions, actively participate by asking thoughtful questions and contributing relevant insights. This shows your engagement and lets others see your interest and expertise in the subject matter.

## Utilize Social Media

Use social media platforms to engage with event hashtags or post updates about the event. Share critical takeaways, tag influential speakers or attendees, and engage in conversations happening online. This will help you expand your network and reach a wider audience.

## *Volunteer or Offer Assistance*

If there are opportunities to volunteer or assist with event organization, seize them. Volunteering shows your commitment to the event and allows you to interact with organizational staff and other influential individuals. This can lead to valuable connections and increased visibility.

## *Follow Up After the Event*

After the event, make sure to follow up with individuals you had meaningful conversations with. Send personalized emails or connect on professional platforms like LinkedIn. This will reinforce the connection made during the event and keep the conversation going.

By implementing these strategies, you can confidently navigate corporate social gatherings with ease. Remember, these events provide valuable opportunities for networking, building relationships, and showcasing your professionalism. As you attend future gatherings, keep these tips in mind to make the most out of every social engagement.

However, even with the best preparation, unforeseen challenges can arise in the corporate world. The next chapter will delve into strategies for handling unexpected setbacks and difficult situations with grace and resilience. Learn how to navigate through tough times and emerge stronger than ever. Get ready to discover valuable insights on what to do when the "wheels come off."

## Chapter 9:
# How to Manage a Personal Crisis Without Derailing Your Corporate Career

*You will never feel truly satisfied by work until you are satisfied by life.*
–Heather Shuck

It's easy to become consumed by our work. As we strive for success and meet the ever-increasing expectations of our professional lives, we often neglect the most important aspect of our existence: life itself. Our careers can often consume us to the point where we forget to focus on our relationships, personal fulfillment, and physical and mental health.

When the relentless pursuit of work takes a toll on our physical and mental health, or when unforeseen circumstances unexpectedly disrupt our carefully planned trajectory, what steps should you take to maintain your career? During these moments of crisis and personal challenge, isolation is not a good strategy. Communicating and tapping corporate resources are necessary to keep your career on track during a personal crisis.

Former Superbowl Champion Michael Strahan has built a very successful media and business career since leaving the NFL. Recently, he announced that his daughter Isabella had a large medulloblastoma—a type of malignant tumor—in her cerebellum. Can you imagine getting that news and having to smile and interview the next guest on *Good Morning America*? I pray every day that Michael Strahan is getting the support he needs. Managing a personal crisis while balancing a corporate career can feel like walking a tightrope over a burning inferno.

The key takeaway of this chapter is a simple-yet-profound truth: Life is more important than work. It may seem obvious, but so many of us get caught in the mindset that our work defines us and is the ultimate measure of our success. However, it is essential to recognize that our work will continue even after we are no longer here. Our employers will reassign our tasks, colleagues will take on our responsibilities, and the business will find a way to carry on.

## Staying Productive When You Have a Personal Crisis

<u>When faced with a personal crisis</u>, maintaining productivity and focusing on work can be incredibly challenging. Personal crises can include a major illness or injury, the loss of a loved one, a relationship breakdown, financial troubles, or any other significant life event that shakes you to your core. In these difficult moments, you need to prioritize self-care and navigate through the crisis in a way that allows

you to heal and find a sense of stability. Here are some strategies to help you stay productive during a personal crisis:

- **Acknowledge and accept your emotions.** Acknowledge and accept your emotions when going through a personal crisis. Allow yourself the time and space to grieve, process, and heal. Suppressing or ignoring your emotions can have a more significant impact in the long run, hindering your productivity. Embrace self-compassion and give yourself permission to feel and experience your emotions fully.

- **Seek support from loved ones.** During a personal crisis, Surround yourself with a strong support network. Reach out to your family, close friends, or a support group to share your feelings and receive emotional support. Communicate your needs clearly, as well as any specific ways in which your loved ones could offer assistance.

- **Communicate with your employer or colleagues.** Open and honest communication with your employer or colleagues is crucial during a personal crisis. Inform them about your situation and any potential impact it may have on your work. This communication helps manage expectations and allows your workplace to provide support and make necessary accommodations.

- **Set realistic and flexible goals.** Recognize that your productivity might be affected during a personal crisis, and that's perfectly normal. Adjust your expectations and set realistic and flexible goals for yourself. Break down tasks into smaller, more manageable chunks, and prioritize the most critical and time-sensitive ones. Consider utilizing time-management techniques such as the Pomodoro Technique, where you work for a set amount of time and then take short breaks.

- **Establish boundaries.** Establishing clear boundaries can help protect your time and space during a crisis. Determine when and where you will dedicate time to work and when you will devote time to self-care and tending to your emotional well-being. This could involve defining specific working hours, turning off notifications outside those hours, and setting expectations with colleagues or managers. Creating these boundaries allows you to maintain a healthier work-life balance and prevent burnout.

- **Practice self-care.** Self-care is crucial during a personal crisis. Engage in activities that help you relax, recharge, and find solace. This includes exercise, mindfulness or meditation practices, journaling, hobbies, leisure time in nature, or seeking therapy or counseling. Prioritizing self-care supports your emotional well-being, builds resilience, and enhances your ability to handle the challenges you're facing.

- **Seek professional help if necessary.** If the personal crisis is affecting your ability to function or cope, consider seeking professional help. Therapists, psychologists, or counselors can provide guidance and support to navigate through challenging times. Their expertise can help you develop coping strategies, process your emotions, and regain a sense of stability, allowing you to become more productive in the long run.

# How to Tell Your Manager You Are Dealing With a Personal Crisis

When facing a personal crisis, informing your manager about the situation can be daunting. However, open and honest communication is essential in maintaining a healthy work environment and obtaining the support you may need during difficult times. Here are some steps to follow when sharing a personal crisis with your manager:

- **Assess your readiness.** Before discussing your crisis with your manager, take some time to assess your readiness and determine if it's the right time to have the conversation. Consider factors such as your emotional stability, the impact of the crisis on your work, and any necessary preparations you need to make before speaking with your manager.

- **Choose the right setting.** Find an appropriate and private setting to have a conversation with your manager. This could be in their office, a meeting room, or any other confidential space where you can have an uninterrupted discussion.

- **Plan what you will say.** Prepare what you want to communicate to your manager before the meeting. Outline the key points you want to convey, including the nature of the crisis, its impact on your ability to work, any changes to your availability or schedule, and any specific assistance or accommodations you might require.

- **Be direct and honest.** When speaking with your manager, be direct and honest about the situation to ensure clear understanding. Provide a brief overview of the personal crisis you are facing, being mindful to disclose only what you are comfortable sharing. Avoid sharing unnecessary personal details that may not be relevant to your work and the support you need.

- **Communicate boundaries and limitations.** Clearly communicate any boundaries or limitations arising from the personal crisis. This could include changes to your working hours, a temporary reduction in workload, or any activities that might require your attention outside of regular work hours. Being transparent about these limitations allows your manager to adjust expectations and provide necessary support or resources.

- **Discuss potential solutions.** Brainstorm potential solutions together with your manager. This could involve adjusting deadlines, reallocating tasks, temporarily reducing your workload, or exploring flexible work options such as remote work or adjusted schedules. Collaborating on potential solutions shows your commitment to finding a balance between your crisis and work responsibilities.

- **Seek support and resources.** Inquire about any available support or resources your organization provides for employees dealing with personal crises. This could include employee-assistance programs, counseling services, or special leave options. Your manager can help guide you to the appropriate resources and ensure you have access to the support you need during this challenging time.

- **Follow up in writing.** After the conversation, consider sending an email to your manager to summarize your discussion. This provides a written record of the understanding reached and any agreed-upon accommodations, ensuring clarity for both parties.

- **Maintain communication.** As you navigate through the personal crisis, maintain open lines of communication with your manager. Inform them of any changes or developments that may impact your work or need for support. Regular updates can help manage expectations and maintain a supportive work environment.

As we've explored various strategies and tips to handle those moments when everything seems to be falling apart, it's important to remember that even the best-laid plans can go awry. The key is learning from our failures and finding the strength to keep moving forward.

As we move forward, the next chapter will examine the crucial topic of leading diverse teams. In today's globalized and multicultural workplace, it's more important than ever to understand the unique challenges faced by individuals from different backgrounds, cultures, and perspectives. Join us as we explore practical strategies and essential skills for effectively leading diverse teams and fostering an inclusive work environment.

## Chapter 10:
# Walk a Mile in Someone's Shoes— How to Lead Diverse Teams

*A diverse mix of voices leads to better discussions, decisions, and outcomes for everyone.*
–Sundar Pichai

This quote encapsulates the core essence of our chapter. By recognizing and valuing the unique perspectives, backgrounds, and experiences diverse team members bring to the company, leaders can unlock the latent potential that lies within their teams.

In today's rapidly evolving and interconnected world, organizations recognize the importance of diverse teams to drive innovation, creativity, and productivity. As more industries become globalized and multicultural, leaders who can effectively navigate the complexities of diverse teams are essential for success. This chapter aims to explore the crucial topic of leading diverse teams, providing valuable insights, practical strategies, and essential skills for fostering inclusivity and maximizing the potential of diversity in the workplace.

## Diversity vs. Difference vs. Woke

Diversity, difference, and woke are interconnected concepts that play a significant role in discussions about inclusivity, equity, and social awareness. While they may seem similar at first glance, each term has a distinct meaning and represents different aspects of creating a more inclusive and equitable society. Let's explore each concept in detail:

### *Diversity*

*Diversity* refers to the range of differences among individuals, including, but not limited to, race, ethnicity, gender, age, sexual orientation, disability, religion, socioeconomic status, and cognitive abilities. It encompasses how people differ, recognizing that each person brings unique perspectives, experiences, and strengths.

The goal of diversity is to challenge traditional norms and create a space where everyone feels valued, respected, and included. By championing diversity, organizations enhance their ability to innovate, problem-solve, and adapt to a rapidly changing world. Embracing diversity is about recognizing the richness that comes from different perspectives and actively working to include and empower individuals from all backgrounds.

### *Difference*

In the context of diversity, *difference* refers to the recognition and celebration of individual and group distinctions. It acknowledges that each person brings their own lived experiences, unique cultural backgrounds, and personal attributes that shape their worldview and perspectives.

Differences can manifest in various forms, such as language, traditions, beliefs, and values. Embracing difference means acknowledging and appreciating the unique characteristics that individuals bring to a group or community. It involves creating spaces where differences are respected and celebrated rather than homogenized or marginalized.

## *Woke*

*Woke* is a term that has gained popularity in recent years, particularly in the social justice and activism arenas. Being woke refers to increased awareness and understanding of social, political, and cultural injustices in society. The term originated within the African American community as a response to systemic racism and police brutality but has since expanded to encompass a broader range of social issues.

Being woke involves being conscious of the privilege and power dynamics that influence our daily lives and actively working to challenge and dismantle those systems of oppression. It is about recognizing that social justice requires ongoing education, self-reflection, and action to address inequality, discrimination, and injustice in all their forms.

The concept of being woke intersects with diversity and difference, as it emphasizes the importance of recognizing and addressing the disparities that exist within society. It promotes a mindset of empathy, compassion, and activism to advocate for equity and justice for marginalized communities.

## Why Diversity Is Essential in Corporate America

Diversity is not just a buzzword or a trend; it is essential for success in corporate America. A diverse workforce brings a multitude of perspectives, experiences, and ideas, which can drive innovation, enhance problem-solving abilities, and lead to better decision-making. In this section, we will explore in detail why diversity is essential in corporate America.

## *Increased Innovation and Creativity*

Diverse teams are more likely to generate innovative ideas and solutions. When people with different backgrounds and perspectives come together, they bring a range of insights and approaches to problem-solving. According to *Forbes Magazine*, "Companies with above-average diversity produced a greater proportion of revenue from innovation (45% of total)" (Levine, 2020). By embracing diversity, corporations can tap into the creativity and potential of their employees, resulting in a competitive advantage in the marketplace.

## *Broader Market Reach*

In a globalized world, diverse teams can better understand and connect with diverse customer bases. By having employees who reflect the demographics of their target markets, companies can build stronger relationships with customers, better understand their needs, and tailor products and services to meet their diverse requirements.

## *Enhanced Decision-Making and Problem-Solving*

Homogeneous groups often suffer from groupthink, where consensus is prioritized over critical thinking. This can limit the quality of decision-making and hinder growth and innovation. Diverse teams bring a wider range of perspectives and ideas. By incorporating diverse viewpoints, companies can engage in more robust and comprehensive discussions that consider a variety of angles. This leads to more informed decisions that consider different risks, opportunities, and potential outcomes.

## Increased Employee Engagement and Retention

Employees are more likely to feel engaged and connected to their work when they can bring their authentic selves to the workplace. A diverse work environment promotes inclusivity and ensures that individuals feel valued and respected for who they are. Employees who feel included and embraced are more likely to be motivated, satisfied, and committed to their work. This, in turn, leads to higher levels of employee retention, reduces turnover costs, and improves overall productivity and efficiency.

## Seeing Through Different Eyes

*Seeing through different eyes* refers to the ability to view situations, problems, and experiences from different perspectives. It is the capacity to understand and empathize with others, stepping into their shoes and <u>seeing the world from their unique vantage point</u>. This mindset of seeing through different eyes is critical for fostering empathy, building inclusive environments, and promoting effective communication and collaboration.

To develop the ability to see through different eyes, it is important to actively seek out diverse perspectives and engage in open and respectful dialogue. This can be done through various means, such as actively listening to others, exposing oneself to diverse sources of information, engaging in cultural-immersion experiences, and seeking feedback from individuals with different backgrounds.

Here are seven ways to start training your eyes to see differently:

- Learn a foreign language.
- Listen to foreign-language radio and music.
- Watch foreign films and TV shows.

- Travel outside your home country. Where possible, stay at local bed & breakfasts.

- Dine at foreign restaurants located in diverse communities.

- Attend cultural festivals and celebrations The more you push yourself outside your comfort zone, the greater your ability to see the world through others' eyes will become.

- Host exchange students.

# How to Lead a Diverse Team—Manager Self-Assessment

Leading a diverse team requires a specific set of skills and competencies to effectively manage and harness the potential of diversity. A manager's readiness to lead a diverse team can be evaluated through a self-assessment that focuses on key areas of diversity management. Below are 20 questions that can test a person's readiness to lead a diverse team:

1. Does an employee's hairstyle determine how productive they will be at work?

2. If a client rejects service from a diverse employee, will you send a different employee to provide the service?

3. Do you shorten employee names (without permission) when they are too difficult to pronounce?

4. Would you appoint a diverse employee to a project team so that the team looks more diverse?

5. Do you make it a point to have one-on-one lunches/coffees with each of your employees?

6. Do you exclude employees from events if they have religious restrictions?

7. Do you exclude employees from events if they have dietary restrictions?

8. Do you plan events that exclude kids?

9. Is your website enabled for the vision impaired?

10. Does your job background screening provider filter for names before generating a list of candidates?

11. Do you offer remote work options for new parents (both mothers and fathers)?

12. Is blue an appropriate hair color for employees?

13. Can employees have exposed tattoos?

14. What percent of your managers are female?

15. What percent of your team was referred by an existing team member?

16. Do you have a process for accepting ideas from all levels of the organization?

17. Is the turnover rate higher for diverse employees than for nondiverse employees?

18. Do you use inside jokes and jargon with a select group of employees?

19. Do the same employees speak at every team meeting?

20. Do you confront gossip and gossipmongers?

By honestly assessing yourself against these questions, you can gauge your readiness and identify areas for growth as a leader of a diverse team. If you answered "no" to more than five of these questions, you should work with your HR staff to find leadership training classes that can address the gaps you face in your organization. If you answered "no" to more than ten of these questions, you will need an expert to help you develop an action plan for change. You need to remember that leading a diverse team requires ongoing commitment, self-reflection, and a willingness to learn and adapt to the unique needs and experiences of team members.

In conclusion, understanding the importance of walking a mile in someone's shoes is essential for leading diverse teams successfully. By embracing empathy, fostering inclusivity, and actively seeking diverse perspectives, we can create environments where every voice is heard and valued.

In the next chapter, we will shift our focus to a different kind of challenge—navigating the delicate process of breaking up with your employer while maintaining a positive relationship. So, prepare as we look into the art of gracefully parting ways in our next chapter.

## Chapter 11:
# How to Breakup With Your Employer and Remain Friends

*If you're brave enough to say goodbye, life will reward you with another hello.*
—Paulo Coehlo

We've all been there at some point in our careers—that moment when you realize it's time to move on from your current employment. Whether due to personal growth, new opportunities, or a desire for change, breaking up with your employer can be challenging and intimidating. But what if we told you it's possible to end your professional relationship on good terms and even remain friends with your employer? Yes, you heard it right—it is indeed possible.

In this chapter, we will delve into the art of parting ways gracefully and preserving positive relationships with your soon-to-be former employer. We will provide valuable insights, strategies, and practical tips on navigating this delicate process while maintaining your network and leaving the door open for future collaborations.

The key takeaway from this chapter is a golden rule of the professional world: Never burn a bridge. We often underestimate the importance of our professional connections and fail to recognize that our career paths may intersect again in the future. Whether through industry events, networking opportunities, or new job prospects, maintaining positive relationships with your former employer can open doors you never thought possible. By breaking up with your employer in a respectful and amicable manner, you increase the chances of leaving a lasting impression and nurturing friendships that can benefit both parties down the road.

# How to Know When It Is Time to Leave Your Company

Knowing when it is time to leave your company can be a difficult decision to make. It is essential to listen to your intuition and pay attention to the signs that indicate it might be time to move on. Here are some factors to consider:

- **Personal growth and development:** One indication that it might be time to leave your company is when you feel stagnant in terms of personal growth and development. If you find yourself doing the same tasks without any new challenges or opportunities for advancement, it can lead to feelings of frustration and lack of motivation. Assess whether your current role aligns with your long-term goals and aspirations (see Chapter 2). If there is little room for growth or learning, it might be a sign that it's time to explore new opportunities elsewhere.

- **Lack of work-life balance:** Another red flag that signals it's time to leave is when your work-life balance is consistently out of balance. Consider whether your current job demands too much of your time and energy without providing enough time for self-care, family, and personal pursuits. If your work-life balance is consistently off-kilter, it may be an indication that it's time to seek a healthier work environment.

- **Unfulfilling work:** Feeling unfulfilled or unsatisfied with your work is a clear sign that it might be time to leave your company. If you wake up each day dreading going to work, feeling unenthusiastic about your tasks, or lacking a sense of purpose, you need to re-read Chapter 2. If you executed the plan in Chapter 2 and still feel unfilled, it may be time to explore other options.

- **Toxic work environment:** A toxic work environment can be detrimental to your mental and emotional well-being. If you experience constant conflicts, unsupportive colleagues or supervisors, office politics, or a generally negative atmosphere, it can significantly impact your job satisfaction and overall happiness. As a first step, report the problems to your boss and human resources. If you find yourself in a toxic work environment that is unlikely to improve, it's time to consider leaving for a healthier and more positive workplace.

- **Company culture and values misalignment:** Misalignment with the company's culture and values can make it challenging to thrive and find fulfillment in your role. If you find yourself disagreeing with the company's values, ethics, or overall direction, it can create a sense of dissonance and lack of purpose. Assess whether your personal values align with the company's values and if there is potential for alignment in the future. If the misalignment is significant and unlikely to change, it may be a clear sign that it's time to seek a company that better aligns with your values.

- **Lack of recognition or appreciation:** Feeling undervalued or underappreciated can be discouraging and demotivating. If your efforts and contributions go unnoticed or unacknowledged, it can erode your job satisfaction and motivation. Before you decide to quit, re-read Chapter 4 and determine whether you have done enough to build and promote your brand. If you consistently feel undervalued despite your best efforts, it may be time to explore opportunities where your contributions are recognized and appreciated.

Ultimately, the decision to leave your company is a personal one that depends on your unique circumstances and goals. Take the time to reflect, assess your current situation, and consult your mentors. Trust yourself and remember that your professional growth and well-being are important. When you recognize the signs that it's time to leave, take the necessary steps to find a new opportunity that aligns with your aspirations and values.

# How to Notify Your Manager When You Are Ready to Quit

Notifying your manager that you are leaving your job can be a difficult and delicate conversation to have. Here are some steps to consider when you are ready to notify your manager:

- **Be prepared.** Before the meeting, be sure to prepare yourself. Write down your honest reasons for leaving, including any feedback or concerns you have about the company or role. It's also important to prepare answers to anticipated questions that your manager might ask you. Remember to stay positive and supportive of your manager during the conversation. Tone is as important as your answers.

- **Schedule an end-of-the-day meeting.** Schedule a one-on-one meeting with your manager to discuss your decision to leave. Schedule the meeting at the end of the work day, which will limit interruptions and give you time to reflect at home.

- **Offer to help.** Show your willingness to help with the transition process. Offer to help train your replacement, provide support in closing out projects, and other help that might be necessary to make the process smoother for your team and your manager.

- **Provide written notice.** After the meeting, provide a formal written notice of your resignation. Your resignation letter should be professional and concise, expressing your gratitude for the opportunities and experiences you have had while working at the company and indicating the last day of your employment.

- **Maintain professionalism.** Throughout the entire process, it's important to maintain professionalism. Avoid sharing negative comments or complaints about the company or colleagues, as it could negatively impact future job opportunities.

- **Follow up.** After providing your notice, it's essential to follow up and confirm the last date of work and any necessary steps related to finalizing your departure. This will help ensure a smooth, positive transition process for you and your employer.

## How to Thank Your Company Mentors Before You Leave

Mentors play an essential role in an individual's professional development and gaining new skills and knowledge in their work. When it's time to move on from your current job, you must take the time to thank your mentors for their guidance and support. Here are some steps you can take to do this effectively:

- **Write a personalized note.** Express your gratitude by writing a sincere, personalized note to your mentors (consider a handwritten note). Highlight specific examples of how they have impacted your career.

- **Offer to stay in touch.** Let your mentor(s) know that you value their connections and would like to stay in touch, even after you leave. Connect on LinkedIn and exchange contact information so that you can reach out to them in the future.

- **Plan to set up a final meeting.** Schedule one last call or meeting with your mentor(s) to thank them in person. This will allow them to share their final advice and gratitude and ensure your professional relationship ends on a positive note.

- **Consider giving a gift.** A small token of appreciation can serve as a nice gesture to show your gratitude. It could be something as simple as flowers or chocolates. Consider giving a custom desk paper weight. This gift will be a constant reminder of your style and class.

Ending your professional relationship with your employer doesn't have to mean burning bridges. By following the steps outlined in this chapter, you can navigate the break-up process with grace and maintain a positive connection with your former employer. Remember: The way you handle this transition can leave a lasting impression on your career reputation and future opportunities.

In the next chapter, we will explore a different journey—transitioning from corporate America to entrepreneurship and the steps you can take to embark on this exciting path.

## Chapter 12:
# You Are Ready to Leave Corporate America to Become an Entrepreneur—What's Your Next Move?

*A desk is a dangerous place from which to view the world.*
—John le Carré

The allure of entrepreneurship is undeniable. The idea of charting your own path, pursuing your passions, and building something from the ground up can be captivating. For individuals who have grown tired of the corporate world's rigidity and limitations, the prospect of leaving corporate America to become an entrepreneur often beckons. It represents a new adventure filled with possibilities and the chance to take control of one's professional destiny.

If you find yourself dreaming about leaving the corporate world and embarking on an entrepreneurial journey, you are not alone. Many individuals yearn for the freedom, creativity, and flexibility of entrepreneurship. However, transitioning from the structure and stability of corporate America to the unpredictable and demanding world of entrepreneurship requires careful planning, strategic thinking, and a clear understanding of the challenges ahead.

This chapter serves as a guide for those who are ready to leap into the world of entrepreneurship. We will explore the essential steps to take, the important considerations to make, and the key decisions that will shape your path as you transition from the corporate boardroom to the world of startups and innovation. Before you take that leap, it is vital to put on your parachute and prepare for the exhilarating, yet risky, journey ahead.

The key takeaway of this chapter is that you need to maximize your corporate perks, relationships, and resources *before* you quit your corporate job.

## Corporate Perks: Join Every Corporate Rewards Program *Before* You Quit Your Job

Please do not quit your corporate job without planning your exit. Successful entrepreneurs either have rich uncles and aunts or they spend a lot of time raising capital to fund their launch. As a corporate employee, you can leverage your corporate perks and relationships to extend your future startup's runway.

Corporate rewards programs offer a range of perks and benefits that can directly impact your bottom line. By joining these programs, you can access discounts, deals, and special offers on various products and services relevant to your business needs. These perks can help you save money on essential expenses such as office supplies, software subscriptions, travel, and accommodations.

As a former corporate executive and business management consultant, I frequently found myself on an airplane headed to meetings with my clients. For ten years, I repeated the weekly cycle of flying to a different city and staying overnight at national chain hotels. When I decided to leave corporate America to launch a biometrics startup, I had one million frequent-flyer miles and hotel-stay points. The money I would have spent on travel for startup was invested in the technology that helped us disrupt the industry. Launching a startup for me was ten years in the making. If you want to follow the same path, take advantage of those corporate perks from day one!

## Soft Launch Your Startup While Maintaining Corporate Job

A soft launch can be a strategic approach to mitigate risks and gain momentum for your new venture. It allows you to test the market, refine your product or service, and build a customer base before fully committing to your startup. Here are some key points to consider when soft launching your startup while maintaining your corporate job:

- **Ethics and conflict of interest:** Ensure no conflicts of interest exist between your corporate job and your startup. Familiarize yourself with any employment agreements, noncompete clauses, or intellectual property rights that may affect your involvement in another business. Adhere to ethical practices and maintain transparency with your employer to avoid any legal or ethical issues.

- **Time management:** Balancing your corporate job and startup requires effective time management. Prioritize tasks, allocate dedicated time slots for your startup, and maintain a schedule to ensure you can handle both commitments without compromising quality or productivity. Be realistic about your available time and set achievable goals for your startup during the soft launch phase.

- **Start small:** Begin with a minimal viable product (MVP) or a simplified version of your offering. This allows you to enter the market quickly and start gathering feedback and data from early customers. As you soft launch, focus on essential features and functionalities while gradually expanding and improving your product based on customer insights and market demands.

- **Validate your idea:** Use the soft launch phase to validate your startup idea and assess market demand. Gather feedback from your initial customers, monitor their usage patterns, and collect data on their preferences and needs. This information will help you refine your product or service, identify potential target markets, and make informed decisions for scaling your startup.

- **Build relationships:** While maintaining your corporate job, leverage your professional network to build relationships with potential partners, customers, or mentors. Attend relevant industry events, join networking groups or communities, and actively engage with relevant stakeholders. These connections can provide valuable support, guidance, and opportunities for your startup's growth during the soft launch phase.

- **Seek support:** Surround yourself with a supportive network or team. Engage with fellow entrepreneurs, join startup incubators or accelerators, or seek mentorship from experienced individuals in your industry. Their insights, advice, and experiences can help you navigate the early stages of your startup while still managing your corporate job.

- **Test marketing and sales strategies:** During the soft launch, experiment with different marketing and sales strategies to understand what works best for your target audience. Utilize social media platforms, create content, engage in influencer marketing, and explore cost-effective advertising options to generate awareness and attract customers. This testing phase will provide insights into customer acquisition costs, conversion rates, and overall market interest.

- **Monitor financials:** While maintaining your corporate job, carefully track and manage your startup's financials. Set a budget and allocate resources wisely. Understand the costs associated with your soft launch and monitor metrics such as revenue, expenses, and cash flow. Being aware of your financial situation will help you make informed decisions about scaling your startup in the future.

- **Transition plan:** As your startup gains traction during the soft launch phase, consider creating a transition plan to move from your corporate job to full-time focus on your startup. Evaluate the feasibility of scaling your startup while maintaining your corporate job, including factors such as financial stability, market potential, and personal circumstances.

- **Self-care:** Managing both a corporate job and a startup can be emotionally and physically demanding. Taking care of your well-being is essential. Prioritize self-care activities such as exercise, sleep, and stress management. Set realistic expectations and seek support from family and friends to maintain a healthy work-life balance.

# Startup Checklist

A startup checklist serves as a guide to help entrepreneurs navigate the complex process of starting a new business. It ensures that crucial steps are not overlooked, increasing the chances of success.

- **Define your business idea.** Clearly define your business idea and identify your target market. Research the industry, competition, and potential customers to validate your concept and understand market opportunities.

- **Conduct market research.** Analyze the market demand, trends, and customer needs to determine whether your business idea is viable. Collect data on competitors, market size, pricing, and customer preferences to make informed decisions.

- **Develop a business plan.** Create a detailed business plan that outlines your objectives, target audience, marketing strategies, financial projections, and operations. This plan will serve as a roadmap for your startup journey and help you secure funding.

- **Determine legal structure.** Decide on the legal structure of your business, such as sole proprietorship, partnership, limited liability company (LLC), or corporation. Consult with legal professionals and determine the necessary licenses, permits, and registrations required for your industry and location.

- **Secure funding.** Determine your startup's financial needs and explore funding options such as personal savings, loans, grants, angel investors, venture capital, or crowdfunding. Prepare a detailed financial plan and pitch deck to present to potential investors or lenders.

- **Build a team.** Identify the key roles and skills needed to run your startup. Recruit a team of talented individuals who share your vision and can contribute to your business's success. Delegate tasks accordingly and establish clear roles and responsibilities. Y-Combinator, the world's most recognizable accelerator, has a [free founder-match marketplace](#) where you can search for co-founders.

- **Create a brand identity.** Develop a compelling brand identity that reflects your business values and resonates with your target audience. Design a logo, choose a color palette, and create consistent visual assets for your website, marketing materials, and social media profiles. Fivver.com is a great platform on which to get a logo designed for less than $10.00.

- **Build a strong online presence.** Create a professional website, register a domain name, and establish a presence on relevant social media platforms. Develop a content strategy to engage with potential customers, build brand awareness, and generate leads.

- **Set up financial systems.** When it comes to your startup financials, start simple. Use simple Excel spreadsheets to build your financials. As you grow, graduate to software packages like Quickbooks. Consult a CPA to help in building your tools. Remember, every dollar you save is a dollar that can extend your startup's runway.

- **Secure insurance.** Assess the insurance needs of your startup and obtain adequate coverage. Common types of insurance include general liability, property insurance, professional liability (errors and omissions), and workers' compensation, depending on your industry and business activities.

- **Develop a sales strategy.** In the early days of a startup, sales are typically founder led. Given this reality, as a potential founder, you should focus on growing the size of your network. Realize that before you have a company brand, your first customers are buying you. The larger the size of your network, the more traction you can get in the early days of your launch.

- **Ensure legal compliance.** Understand the legal and regulatory requirements specific to your industry and location. Comply with tax obligations, data-protection laws, employment regulations, and other relevant regulations to avoid legal issues and penalties.

- **Monitor and evaluate.** Continuously monitor and evaluate your startup's performance against key performance indicators (KPIs) and milestones. Make data-driven decisions, identify areas for improvement, and adjust your strategies accordingly.

As you take the first step toward your entrepreneurial journey, remember to always stay hungry, humble, and willing to learn. The path might be tough, but with hard work and determination, success is attainable. As we approach the end of this book, get ready to take your business to soaring heights!

# Conclusion

As we come to the end of this book, you'll need to equip yourself with the necessary resources and tools to navigate your career journey. Here are a few things to remember as you venture into corporate America.

## Resources for New Corporate Employees

Starting a new job can be both exciting and overwhelming. Fortunately, there are resources available to help make the transition smoother.

- **Alignable: Business Networking Platform:** https://www.alignable.com/—A network for more than 8.5 million business owners

- **Clubhouse:** https://www.clubhouse.com—A social audio networking app

- **LinkedIn:** https://www.linkedin.com—A business and employment-focused social media platform

- **LunchClub:** https://lunchclub.com/—A one-on-one virtual networking platform

## Mental Health Resources

Maintaining good mental health is essential for career success and overall well-being. Organizations are increasingly recognizing the importance of mental health and providing resources to support their employees. Many companies offer employee assistance programs

(EAPs) that provide confidential counseling services and mental health resources. Here are some additional resources and articles you should review:

- **Awareness:** https://itunes.apple.com/us/app/awareness/id402123427?mt=8—Connect with your emotional intelligence

- **Calm:** https://www.calm.com—Immerse yourself in Calm's soothing music and sounds made for sleep, focus and relaxation

- **HeadSpace:** https://www.headspace.com/—Unlock self-care ideas that stick, even when you're busy

- How to stay productive at work when a personal crisis Is taking over your life: https://www.themuse.com/advice/how-to-stay-productive-at-work-when-a-personal-crisis-is-taking-over-your-life

- National Suicide Prevention Lifeline at 1-800-273-TALK (8255), or call or text 988

- **Sleep Cycle:** https://www.sleepcycle.com/—Wake up feeling well-rested

- What to do when a personal crisis is hurting your professional life: https://hbr.org/2017/11/what-to-do-when-a-personal-crisis-is-hurting-your-professional-life

# Career and Leadership Book Recommendations

Reading books that provide insights into career development and leadership can be instrumental in shaping your professional growth (Munro, 2023). Here are some recommended titles:

- *The Art of Possibility* by Rosamund Stone Zander and Benjamin Zander—This book encourages a shift in mindset and provides tools for unlocking creativity and embracing new possibilities

- *Body of Work: Finding the Thread That Ties Your Story Together* by Pamela Slim

- *David & Goliath: Underdogs, Misfits, and the Art of Battling Giants* by Malcolm Gladwell

- *Die Empty: Unleash Your Best Work Every Day* by Todd Henry

- *The Mentor Leader: Secrets to Building People and Teams That Win Consistently* by Tony Dungy

- *Presence: Bringing Your Boldest Self to Your Biggest Challenges* by Amy Cudd

- *Think Like a Monk* by Jay Shetty—A transformative journey that invites you to rewire your mind for lasting peace and purpose

- *The 7 Habits of Highly Effective People* by Stephen Covey—This book provides a framework for achieving goals, building meaningful relationships, and prioritizing what truly matters

- "9 Ways to Evaluate Just How Valuable You Are at Work": https://www.themuse.com/advice/9-ways-to-evaluate-just-how-valuable-you-are-at-work

- "10 Ways to Show Your Value as an Employee": https://www.inc.com/martin-zwilling/10-ways-to-show-your-value-as-an-employee.html

These books offer valuable perspectives and strategies for professional development and leadership growth. As a lifelong learner, incorporating them into your reading list will further enhance your career journey.

# Startup Resources

For those aspiring to become entrepreneurs or venture into the world of startups, having access to valuable resources is crucial. Here are some books and resources that will make you smarter as an entrepreneur:

- Alignable: Business Networking Platform: https://www.alignable.com/—Network for more than 8.5 million business owners

- BeeKonnected: https://beekonnected.com/—A virtual community made up entirely of entrepreneurs who want to grow impactful relationships and expand their online presence

- B2BeeMatch: https://B2BeeMatch.com/—Connect with the B2B companies you need to scale your business

- ClickUp CRM: www.clickup.com—Free CRM for startups

- A Comprehensive Guide to Startup Fundraising: **https://t.ly/USyWc** —A comprehensive and actionable resource that equips founders and entrepreneurs with the knowledge and strategies needed to excel at every stage of the fundraising journey

- Facebook: https://www.facebook.com/—With more than 2 billion active users, Facebook gives startups the potential to reach over 25% of people on the planet

- Fiverr: https://www.Fiverr.com—Connects freelancers to people or businesses looking to hire

- *Guerrillapreneur: Small Business Strategy for Davids Looking to Defeat Goliath*, by Mark Anthony Peterson—Provides entrepreneurs ways to soft launch their startups and win market niches

- Hivebrite: https://www.hivebrite.com/—Entrepreneur networking platform

- *Sell More Faster: The Ultimate Sales Playbook for Startups*, by Amos Schwartzfarb—Guide for entrepreneurs seeking product-market fit, building their sales team, developing a growth strategy, and chasing accelerated, sustained selling success

- Wix: https://www.Wix.com—Create and publish a free website for your business

- Y Combinator Co-Founder Matching: https://www.ycombinator.com/cofounder-matching—A free resource for finding a co-founder

- Y-Combinator Startup School: https://www.startupschool.org/—A free online course on how to start a startup

- Competitive Analysis Worksheet: https://t.ly/h8kmR - designed to help you organize the data you need to make educated guesses about each of your competitors' strategic intent and options

- Sample Non-Disclosure Agreement (NDA): https://t.ly/MVCbE - An NDA is a legal agreement which defines information that the parties wish to protect from dissemination and outlines restrictions on use.

- Financial Statement Starter Kit: https://t.ly/xfA-L - Excel templates that let you track your revenues, and expenses.

- Business Plan Guide - https://t.ly/Vn_pM - Template that helps you write your startup's business plan.

- 6 Free Business Budget Templates: https://t.ly/8-Tni

# Glossary

- **Burnout:** A state of chronic physical and emotional exhaustion, often resulting from prolonged stress and overwork, affecting one's ability to perform effectively.

- **Career coaching:** A process of providing guidance and support to individuals in their career development, helping them identify goals, overcome obstacles, and make informed decisions.

- **Corporate America:** The world of large corporations and business environments associated with traditional office jobs and hierarchical organizational structures.

- **Corporate culture:** The shared values, beliefs, and behavior patterns that characterize an organization, influencing how employees interact and make decisions.

- **Decision-making:** The process of evaluating available options and selecting the best course of action based on thorough analysis and consideration of potential consequences.

- **Emotional intelligence:** The ability to recognize, understand, and manage one's emotions, and the emotions of others, often considered an essential skill in a professional setting.

- **Entrepreneurship:** The process of starting and managing a business, often involving innovation, risk-taking, and creating value in the market.

- **Feedback:** Constructive criticism or input provided by others to help individuals improve their performance and make necessary changes.

- **Goal-setting:** The process of defining and planning specific objectives to be achieved, creating a roadmap for personal and professional success.

- **Leadership:** The ability to guide, inspire, and motivate others toward a common goal while effectively managing resources and making strategic decisions.

- **Mentor:** An experienced and trusted advisor who provides guidance and wisdom to a less-experienced individual, helping them navigate their career path.

- **Networking:** The act of establishing and nurturing professional relationships with individuals in one's industry or field, with the intention of expanding one's professional circle and creating opportunities.

- **Personal branding:** The process of crafting and managing one's reputation, expertise, and image to differentiate oneself from others and create a unique, professional identity.

- **Proactive:** Taking initiative and responsibility for one's actions rather than simply reacting to situations or waiting for things to happen.

- **Professional development:** Activities and processes undertaken to enhance one's knowledge, skills, and competencies related to their profession or field of work.

- **Resilience:** The ability to bounce back from setbacks and adapt to changes in the workplace, demonstrating mental toughness and a positive attitude.

- **Self-reflection:** The practice of introspection and self-analysis, allowing individuals to understand their strengths, weaknesses, and areas for growth.

- **Time management:** The practice of planning and organizing one's time effectively, prioritizing tasks, and increasing productivity.

- **Work-life balance:** The concept of maintaining a healthy equilibrium between one's professional obligations and personal life, ensuring sufficient time and energy for both.

# References

*BrainyQuote.* (2019). BrainyQuote; BrainyQuote. https://www.brainyquote.com/quotes/albert_einstein_121993

*Consulting.* (2023). 47 case interview examples (from McKinsey, BCG, Bain, etc.). IGotAnOffer. https://igotanoffer.com/blogs/mckinsey-case-interview-blog/case-interview-examples

Johnson, C., Beiman, I., & Thompson, J. (n.d.). *Introduction to the Balanced Scorecard and Performance Measurement Systems Balanced Scorecard for State-Owned Enterprises Driving Performance and Corporate Governance.* https://www.adb.org/sites/default/files/publication/29027/balanced-scorecard.pdf

Karrass, C. (1996, January 1). *In Business As In Life- You Don't Get What You Deserve,....* Goodreads. https://www.goodreads.com/en/book/show/921113

Levine, S. R. (2020, January 15). *Diversity Confirmed To Boost Innovation And Financial Results.* Forbes. https://www.forbes.com/sites/forbesinsights/2020/01/15/diversity-confirmed-to-boost-innovation-and-financial-results/?sh=10e1df0c4a6a

Lewis, G. (2023). *10 Unexpected Interview Questions to Get Unrehearsed Answers.* LinkedIn. https://www.linkedin.com/business/talent/blog/talent-acquisition/unexpected-interview-questions-to-get-unrehearsed-answers

Lopez, A. L. (2023, October 5). *Importance of Networking.* University Lab Partners. https://www.universitylabpartners.org/blog/importance-of-networking#:~:text=Why%20Should%20You%20Conduct%20Networking

Massachusetts Institute of Technology. (2022, June 13). *Using the STAR method for your next behavioral interview* (worksheet included). Career Advising & Professional Development | MIT. https://capd.mit.edu/resources/the-star-method-for-behavioral-interviews/

Munro, I. (2023, January 13). *Best Leadership Books: 29 of the Most Impactful Reads*. BetterUp. https://www.betterup.com/blog/best-leadership-books

Out, S. G. (2023, July 27). *Why Emotional Intelligence is a Critical Leadership Skill*. She+ Geeks Out. https://www.shegeeksout.com/blog/why-emotional-intelligence-is-a-critical-leadership-skill/#:~:text=Emotional%20intelligence%20plays%20a%20huge%20role%20in%20effective%20leadership.&text=Emotionally%20intelligent%20leaders%20possess%20a

*The 4 "C's" of Well Designed Meetings*. (n.d.). Navalent. https://www.navalent.com/resources/blog/the-4-cs-of-well-designed-meetings/

www.ingramcontent.com/pod-product-compliance
Lightning Source LLC
Chambersburg PA
CBHW050306230526
45471CB00005B/2051